APNA TIME AAYEGA

INSPIRING STORIES OF MUMBAI'S GRASSROOTS YOUTH

APNA TIME AAYEGA

INSPIRING STORIES OF MUMBAI'S GRASSROOTS YOUTH

Curated & Edited
by

Aaditya Sengupta Dhar
Founder, Project Kahaani

Presented by *Project Kahaani* in collaboration with Udaan India Foundation

Anecdote
Publishing House
For the love of quality reading!

Anecdote
Publishing House
For the love of quality reading!

anecdotepublishinghouse.com
champreaders.com

Anecdote Publishing House
2nd Floor 2/15 Lane no. 2 Ansari Road, Daryaganj-110002
Email: info@anecdotepublishinghouse.com
Website: anecdotepublishinghouse.com

Published by Anecdote Publishing House

First Edition 2025
ISBN 978-81-982589-1-5
MRP ₹ 350/-

Book Promoted and Marketed by Champ Readers Pvt. Ltd.
Edited by:- Aaditya Sengupta Dhar
Cover design by:- Rishikumar Thakur
Layout by:- Arivazhagi Balasundaram
Printed by Thomson Press (India) Ltd, New Delhi

CONTENTS

Introduction by the Editor vii

Foreword by the Founder & CEO, Udaan India Foundation xv

The stories of Apna Time Aayega 1

About Udaan India Foundation 214

About Project Kahaani 216

About Aaditya Sengupta Dhar 218

INTRODUCTION BY THE EDITOR

When I was very young, I learned that we live in a nation called India.

As I grew older, I realised that there is not one India, but two.

I grew up in Mumbai, the city where this reality constantly confronts you. The city where skyscrapers cast their long shadows over sprawling slums; the city where, as I rode down the road on my bus to school every day, I saw children my age playing on the sidewalks in front of cramped houses and wearing tattered clothes. This always struck me as unfair and unnatural, though I was not fully able to grasp the complex issues of the society around me. My friends and I were largely insulated in our world, and the moments when I gave thought to the world outside, to the society at large, and the lives of others like me born into different backgrounds, were only too sporadic.

Then came the COVID lockdowns. The world changed, our lives changed, and how I related to the world around me changed.

I would awake to the sights on television and the internet of endless trains of people trekking under the scorching heat, with weary eyes and limbs, women bearing babies on their shoulders.

I heard that they were migrant workers, forced to return to their homes during the lockdown, having been deserted by the 'city of dreams' to which they had come seeking opportunity and a better life. The sight of these families made me think more deeply about the experiences of these people, who seemed much like my family but were being forced to endure vastly different circumstances. I had always had a passion for writing and had written two fantasy novels by then. I was only twelve years old at that time, but I remember thinking about whether I needed to write about fantastic worlds born out of imagination, when in front of me was unfolding a dystopia, one where those unfortunate to be born into humble beginnings were being further crushed under the weight of a natural pandemic and of a man-made society which had no place for people like them.

Surely, they deserved a chance, didn't they?

As I read more, I realised that being born into humble beginnings did not condemn people to a life of poverty and destitution. There have been many who have dared to dream of rising above these beginnings and have succeeded and made a name for themselves – people like Abdul Kalam, Narayana Murthy, and Milkha Singh. This realisation gave birth to *Underdogs: Legends with Humble Beginnings*, a book that shared the stories of twelve famous people who came from humble beginnings and discussed the importance of helping underprivileged children unleash their potential. I donated all sales proceeds to Save the Children India. It was a humble contribution by a young child, but giving away all I earned from my writing to a cause I was passionate about was one of the high points of my life.

This experience made me reflect more deeply about those who are denied opportunities and still strive to achieve great things in life. In many ways, it changed the way I looked at the society around me; and how I looked at the obvious disparities in my city and in the streets around my house.

My desire to learn more about how to make a difference, and to educate myself about the causes of the inequalities I saw around me, led me to do an internship at UNICEF. I got grounding both in the complexities of the social and economic issues that lead to inequality in our society, and also the many ways in which ordinary people could make a difference. Under the mentorship of a senior UNICEF leader, I wrote my next book, *The Teen's Guide to Saving the World,* sharing stories of real teens making a difference to their communities, and how, with everyday steps we could all take to positively impact the world we will inherit as adults.

As I grew older, as a student of History and Economics in High School, I read more about why and how our society has evolved the way it has, and what it means for our collective future. I learned that India is the world's fastest-growing major economy, with dreams of rising to new heights and becoming a great global economic superpower. I also learned how its young human resources were seen as the essential fuel for an unparalleled demographic dividend. A dividend accrued from a large young workforce, with 600 million Indians between the ages of 18 and 35, whose collective ambition, dreams, and effort could power the economy for decades to come and be the key to the nation's success. However, as I dug deeper, I found that these people were more than just part of the vast 'demographic dividend' – they were people with their own stories, and these stories were, unfortunately, often tinged by bitterness and disappointment.

According to the International Monetary Fund, in India, college graduates are nine times more likely to be unemployed than the illiterate. Youth, seeing education as the ticket to a better life, toil for years to secure a better future for their families and themselves, only to be let down by an education system that does not equip them with the necessary skills and a society that sees, as the World Economic Forum finds, nine out of ten of them *unemployable*. They complete degrees in colleges that are often poorly staffed, equipped and managed, leaving them with no real qualifications; or they find that the newest AI model has taken the jobs that they had been dreaming of for years; or that, in the three or four years they took to get their degrees, society has come to value cutting-edge skills that were not in vogue when they began their college education. Also, as is all too common for those from humble backgrounds, degrees and mark sheets do not equip them with soft skills such as communication that are often critical to get, and thrive in, jobs in the real world outside the cocoon of their classrooms.

Who gives voice to the stories of these young people? The media around us is full of celebrities, sports stars, and business tycoons. Who tells the stories of these youth from the 'other India' who aspire to improve their lives and those of their families, but find the path to their dreams blocked by numerous obstacles? Who tells the stories of the real youth behind the number that marks India's 'demographic dividend'? Who tells the stories of those youth who may not live in the echo chamber of air-conditioned boardrooms and newsrooms that form much of the media narrative, but are the 'real India', with close to seventy per cent of Mumbai's population living in slums and tenements?

As a child looking out at the world during the lockdown, I had wondered how I could help other kids who were not born with the privileges and opportunities that many around me took for granted. Now, as an older teen, and with the desire to not just write about it, but to make a more tangible difference, I thought of how I could get more involved. I had read *Ikigai* and wanted to combine my passion for storytelling with the need I saw around me of giving voice to the stories, dreams, and hopes of these youth and of equipping them with communication skills beyond what they learned in textbooks.

This was how the idea for *Project Kahaani* (story in Hindi) was born. A project devoted to giving voice to these youth through the power of storytelling and equipping them with the communication skills that come with storytelling, to help supplement their classroom knowledge and set them up for success in the real world of work.

I had spent ten years living in Powai in Mumbai, and from the balcony of our apartment, I would sometimes see groups of children gathering on the grounds of a nearby school. Once, I visited one such event and learned that it was a Sports Day, organised by the Udaan India Foundation, which worked with local children from slums and low-income families to help with their education and skill development. I learned more about the work they had done for many years in the local community, and when I thought of *Project Kahaani*, Udaan seemed like the natural partner to reach out to.

Here was an organisation that did not just extend help to those in need, but mentored and nurtured children at every stage of their development, from their nascent years to their graduation, constantly guiding, inspiring, and upskilling them to make sure they had support so that they could face the challenges of the world with competence, confidence and a sense of clear purpose. I spoke to Mamta Ma'am, the founder, to learn more about Udaan. The more I learned, the more I realised this could be the perfect match for what I wanted to do – work with fellow teens and see how I could be of service to them.

She invited me to go to the Udaan centre in Powai to meet the youth, get to know them, and discuss my initiative with them. When I went there, one of the first things I realised was that while, on the face of it, our lives may have been very different, we had much in common. As I spoke to them, I felt not like an outsider but as one of them. That day, many of them volunteered to share their own stories with everyone in the room, with an openness and courage that was inspiring. Hearing them tell their stories made me feel, for the first time, that I was not a distant observer of issues or a teller of stories about issues. I was part of this story.

As I heard teenagers of my age share their lives and dreams, I could empathise with them, with their desire to spread their wings and soar, to unlock the dreams they held close to their chest. When I spoke to them about the *Kahaani* initiative and the idea of expressing their stories through open letters, their eyes lit up, for they saw this as a chance to share their voices with the world. It was amazing how Udaan seemed to have created such a supportive yet charged atmosphere that felt like, it brought out the best in all of these teenagers. At the end of it, together we proclaimed, *Apna Time Aayega!* What better way of bringing their collective voices to life through their stories than to confidently proclaim that indeed, our time will come one day.

This is a project of teens, by teens. I have written books earlier, but for me, this was a new experience, to not be the writer or storyteller, but to be the one helping others tell their stories. Through the many workshops we did together, to help them with storytelling skills and writing and the countless WhatsApp messages in our group, I am grateful to all of these new friends for having embraced me as one of their own, for sharing their stories with me, and for giving me the privilege and opportunity to bring their stories to you.

As you read these open letters, I hope you are inspired by how Ashish overcame the turmoil of a life-threatening condition, bouncing back with an entrepreneurial zeal to improve the lives of his family. I hope you root for Aaryan, working as a delivery boy to pay off his family's debts, never losing the smile on his face or his passion for rapping. I hope you exult with Shalini as she overcomes repeated disappointments to work towards her dream of becoming a CA.

I am grateful to Mamta Ma'am and Sushree Ma'am of Udaan, for bringing me into the Udaan family and partnering with *Project Kahaani*. Mr. Sagar Azad at Anecdote Publishing, has been a pillar of support and encouragement and is the reason you are holding this book in your hands. Finally, I'm ever thankful to my parents, for always teaching me that being a good person is more important than just being a good student and that the best use of one's passions and talents is to be of service to others.

In this book are the voices and the stories of a few dozen of these remarkable teens I had the opportunity to work with, but they are a microcosm of the millions of young adults out there, full of dreams and aspirations, looking for the opportunity to be heard. I hope you don't stop at just reading these stories.

Get involved.

Find your own *Ikigai.* Don't stop at just clicking 'donate' on a website button but get to know these amazing youth behind that website. Get to know the people behind the stories. Mentor them, coach them, and help them get the opportunities they deserve.

We are India's youth, these are our stories, and we are confident that with your support, apna time aayega!

Aaditya Sengupta Dhar

FOREWORD BY THE FOUNDER & CEO, UDAAN INDIA FOUNDATION

Dear Readers,

As I sit down to write this foreword, I am reminded of the boundless potential that lies within every child. Yet millions find their futures prescribed by the lottery of birth, denied the basic right to quality education and opportunity. It was this conviction that led us to start Udaan India Foundation, a non-profit organisation dedicated to empowering children from underserved communities to reach their full potential.

Our mission is built on the belief that every child deserves access to quality education, equal opportunities, and unwavering support, regardless of their socio-economic background. We strive to create an emotionally-safe and a nurturing space where children can grow, learn, and thrive. We envision a space where children dare to dream, and where someone dares to believe! By providing holistic quality education, we aim to unlock the unique potential of each child and empower them to become change-makers in their communities. Over the past two decades, we have had the privilege of walking alongside thousands of young minds, nurturing their aspirations, and empowering them to shape their own futures. We have witnessed countless stories of sacrifices, triumphs, hopes, resilience, and determination.

Apna Time Aayega, curated by young author Aaditya Sengupta Dhar, who started *Project Kahaani*, and reached out to collaborate with us, is a celebration of the stories of some of our youth who have walked or are still walking the Udaan journey. As part of our 20-year celebrations, we were keen to give voice to the stories of our youth who are Udaan's raison d' etre.

When Aaditya reached out to us with *Project Kahaani*, I knew it was not a mere coincidence. Aaditya's interaction with our youth was truly remarkable. He shared his own story and vision for *Project Kahaani*, and listened with empathetic ears to their stories of struggles and triumphs. In those moments of sharing, we witnessed the true spirit of India –where social anxieties and socio-economic backgrounds melted and young India's dreams took centre stage. And Aaditya's empathy, sensitivity and passion for storytelling brought their stories to life in a delightful way, capturing the essence of their journeys and the transformative power of education and empowerment.

As you read these pages, you will discover the dreams, aspirations and hopes of our youth. You will meet Santoshi, who makes you believe dreams do come true; Rupa, who reminds you that all it takes to change a life is someone who believes in you; and Preeti, who urges you to take control of your destiny. You will also meet Dhananjay, who rose from a construction site to become a successful entrepreneur; Rajan, who once juggled two jobs and college and is now an Oracle consultant; and Ganga who dares to become a model and represent India on a global stage!

Each story in this book represents thousands more waiting to be written. They show us that dreams don't have pin codes, that determination can rewrite destinies, and that education is the greatest equaliser. Through their voices, you'll understand why Udaan isn't just a foundation – it's a movement of hope, a catalyst for change, and for many, a home.

These stories live within us, drive us and inspire us every day. And as you turn the pages, I hope you too will be inspired, to challenge your assumptions, to give wings to your unfulfilled dreams, and to sprinkle hope in your life. As you embark on creating your own stories of change around you, we at Udaan look forward to being a part of your journey!

With unwavering hope and gratitude

Mamta Rangan

THE STORIES OF 'APNA TIME AAYEGA'

Presented in these pages are the stories of youths who participated in this project. All these young people have some things in common.

Yes, they all live in Mumbai. Most, if not all of them, lived at some time in the Powai area, where their families came in search of better prospects, often from faraway villages.

They all benefitted from the guidance and care of the Udaan India Foundation, and they all agreed to be part of this collaboration with *Project Kahaani*, to bring their stories to the world.

Their stories are all told through open letters, proclaiming to you, the reader, and the world at large, their hopes, aspirations, and the inspiring journeys they have been on.

However, these youth have something much more fundamental in common – their hope for a better tomorrow, and their drive and determination to make that tomorrow happen. Together, these youth herald a bright future not only for themselves but for our society and country as a whole, a future which they approach with enthusiasm and conviction that, no matter where we start or the obstacles in the way, our time will indeed come!

DHANANJAY'S STORY

Dear Reader,

Before sharing more about myself, I would like to give a short summary of my family. I live in a big family of five brothers, three sisters, and my mom. All of us are well-educated now. My family has a merchant navy officer, a psychologist, two teachers, a tailor, and a career counsellor – me. All of us owe our success to the Udaan India Foundation. My parents were migrants who had come to Bombay in search of a livelihood. We used to live at a construction site in Hiranandani, Powai.

It was a hard life at times, and there wasn't always enough money for all our needs. However, while we may have been poor financially, my parents impressed upon us the importance of having in abundance a thirst for education and knowledge.

When I joined Udaan, I was a very shy child. I remember my mom pinning a handkerchief to my brother and my pockets and combing our hair on the first day I ventured out. The teachers at Udaan, especially Jagruti Didi (my KG teacher) were very warm and appreciative. This made us students very comfortable, which in turn made learning more enjoyable. My parents might not have had the best education themselves, but they knew the power of hard work, and they ensured those values were passed on to us and applied in the pursuit of our studies. In the 1st standard, my brother and I got a scholarship from Udaan and were admitted to an English medium school in our area. We were also tutored by Miss Choo from Singapore, who taught us English. This allowed us to participate and win in a lot of competitions.

After school, I graduated with a degree in Physics from college. While pursuing my degree, I did my NCC (a three-year course in the youth wing of the Indian armed forces). I also joined an NGO as an operations executive. In due time, I also became a social media content executive. During my five years at the NGO, I led a team of members and interns in a variety of segments such as event execution, fundraising, content creation, vendors' contact, and training. It was during this time, through all these experiences, that my will to serve society got stronger.

After completing my degree (2021), I joined an NGO as a part-time career counsellor. During my two years as a career counsellor, I learned a lot of new things in the education sector.

I have juggled a lot of jobs and ideas in my quest to learn new things, as I believe curiosity keeps us young. It has been quite hectic many times, but in the end, the results are always worth the effort. I've always believed in a quote by Harvey Dent (movie character) from *Batman*.

He said, 'The night is the darkest before the dawn', and this has always kept me going.

At present, I am preparing for the civil services examination. I do a part time job, manage my own finances, work on my own business and volunteer with many NGOs. I aspire to become an IAS officer and serve the people by being a part of the government.

My journey began at a construction site, and perhaps there are many kids like me who may never get the opportunities I did and whose destiny is determined by their background, not their talent or dreams. I am lucky that I had parents who encouraged me and mentors like my teachers at Udaan who helped me see my potential. Next time you see a child on the street, or the slum, or a construction site, don't judge them by their surroundings or background. Try and help them achieve their potential.

As Albert Einstein said, 'Every child is special. But if you judge a fish by its ability to climb a tree, it will spend its whole life believing that it is stupid'.

Regards,
Dhananjay

Aayushi's Story

Dear Reader,

I am a teenager from the vibrant city of Mumbai, where every street tells a story, and every corner holds a dream. As I pen down this letter, I am filled with a mix of excitement and introspection, eager to share a glimpse of my journey with you.

Growing up in Mumbai, I've always been surrounded by an atmosphere of boundless energy and ambition. This city has been the backdrop of my dreams and aspirations. From the bustling markets to the serene beaches, each experience has shaped my perspective and fuelled my passion for knowledge and innovation. My dream is to harness the power of technology to make a meaningful impact in the world. With a keen interest in data science and artificial intelligence, I aspire to become an engineer who goes beyond the traditional 9-to-5 role. I envision myself leading my own start-up, driving innovation, and creating solutions that can transform lives. At the age of 17, I am already working on my own start-up, determined to pave my own path and build something truly impactful.

But the road to where I am today has been anything but smooth. Let me take you through my story, which is as much about dreams as it is about the hurdles that come along the way. It's a tale of discovering passions, overcoming obstacles, and finding inspiration in the most unexpected places.

I was just five-years-old when I was admitted to a local municipal corporation school in my area. The atmosphere there was anything but conducive to learning; teachers were more interested in gossiping than teaching, leaving students to fend for themselves. I was a quiet girl, not one to speak up or stand out. A year later, I was promoted to the 2nd standard, and it was then that my father, through a friend, got to know about Udaan India Foundation, a non-profit organisation. My father enrolled me and my two elder sisters there, and that decision marked the beginning of a new chapter in my life.

At Udaan, I met Nadani and Kartik Bhaiya, who became my close companions. The same year, I also formed a girls' group with three other friends. While I was an average student academically, scoring above passing marks but not quite reaching the top, Udaan introduced me to extracurricular activities that I had never experienced before. These activities brought a new sense of joy and excitement into my life. I was content in my quiet way, enjoying my time at Udaan, until one day, a teacher, or *didi* as we called them, complained to my mother about my lack of participation in class. That moment stung, but it also ignited a change in me. The same Didi later became my class teacher and discovered how mischievous I could be. Despite being labelled an average student, I found ways to have fun and make the most of my time at Udaan.

As the years passed, Saturdays became synonymous with the joy of Udaan's clubs, and I even

harboured dreams of becoming a photographer after learning about photography in the 7th standard.

But life had more changes in store for me. I entered the 8th standard and switched to a new, Hindi-medium private school. The experience was jarring; the teachers in this new school actually taught each subject, and each subject had a different teacher. It was a shock, but over time, I adjusted.

Then, the lockdown happened. The world as we knew it changed, and suddenly, my siblings and I were spending all our time together. We cooked, played games, and made the most of our time indoors. School went online, and I confess, I took those lectures for granted, thinking I could just coast through my 9th standard with the same mindset. I even believed that my 10th Board exams would be online, where I could easily copy my way through. But reality had other plans.

When the lockdown lifted and schools reopened, I was faced with a daunting challenge. My elder sister had scored 91% in her 10th standard, setting a high benchmark in our family. My brother aimed to surpass it but fell short. Now, all eyes were on me. Deep down, I knew I was just an average student, but I couldn't bring myself to tell my parents. The pressure was immense, and I was terrified of disappointing them.

Udaan was still operating online, and I felt lost without the support I used to receive there. But I am forever grateful to my brother, who took it upon himself to tutor me. His dedication inspired me, and I began to study harder than ever before, putting in six to eight hours a day –

an enormous effort for someone who had always considered herself average.

My efforts paid off in small but meaningful ways. I was chosen as the class monitor, a role that filled me with pride. I knew the struggles of the backbenchers and did my best to shield my classmates from trouble. My class teacher was delighted with me, and for a while, everything seemed to be falling into place. But inside, I was still battling my insecurities.

When the Board exams finally arrived, I faced them with newfound confidence. I gave my best, and soon, it was time for the results. That moment was a whirlwind of emotions – confusion, fear, nervousness, and tears all at once. My eldest sister called to tell me that I had scored 90%. Instead of celebrating, I broke down in tears. They weren't tears of joy; they were tears of disappointment for not scoring 91%.

The thought of facing my parents with anything less than their expectations crushed me. I even had fleeting thoughts of ending it all, but I didn't. My parents, though not overjoyed, smiled for me, and I took comfort in that. Still, the pain lingered, and I kept it to myself, not sharing my true feelings with anyone.

As I moved forward, it was time to choose my future. I decided to pursue a diploma in engineering, a choice that came with its own set of challenges. Everyone assumes that the youngest child is pampered, but I found the opposite to be true. As the youngest, I felt I had to grow up faster. My parents, having already gone through the milestones with my elder siblings, seemed less concerned with mine. I was left to manage on my own.

In my first year of college, I started teaching students from first to 5th standards at home. Balancing college and teaching were tough, and I struggled to enjoy my teenage years. The language barrier was another hurdle – having come from a Hindi medium background, I found it hard to follow lectures in English. I often cried alone in the bathroom, feeling like a failure as a daughter, a teacher, and a sister. My first-semester results reflected my struggles. I scored only 78%, a far cry from the 91% I had aimed for. It was a low point, and I felt utterly discouraged. But once again, I picked myself up, determined to manage my time better and improve.

My second semester went more smoothly, and a glimmer of hope arrived when I secured my first internship at a multinational company, thanks to Udaan. Despite being the youngest intern, I earned the nickname 'Chhota Packet Bada Dhamaka' for my contributions. My experience at Abbott, where I was the youngest intern, remains one of the most cherished memories of my life. The positive feedback I received boosted my confidence, and I returned to college with a renewed sense of purpose.

However, not all was well. I experienced my first friendship breakup, a painful experience that left me questioning myself. My best friend and I had a fallout in August 2023, and her parting words, calling me selfish, cut deep. I cried silently in the washroom, hiding my pain from everyone. But I learned an important lesson from that experience – no one will always be there for you, and you must learn to stand strong on your own.

As the year went on, I continued to manage my life without the help I once relied on. My professors often scolded me, and I felt like a failure as a student. But the challenges only strengthened my resolve. Although I missed out on extracurricular activities due to my college schedule, I stayed connected with Udaan, sharing my achievements with them and finding solace in their pride. Despite the setbacks, I managed to reclaim my place among the top students by the fifth semester, securing the fifth rank in my class. This achievement was a testament to my hard work and perseverance, and I'm determined to continue striving for excellence.

Through all the ups and downs, I've come to realise that life is a series of tests, each one teaching us how to stand stronger, dream bigger, and rise above our challenges. The most important lesson I've learnt is to embrace my journey, with all its highs and lows. To my young readers, I have this to say: learn to live alone, manage your feelings, and navigate your hardships because not everyone will understand what you're going through. Keep your struggles and triumphs close to your heart until you find someone who truly supports you.

This is the age when you will face some of your toughest challenges, but it's also the age where you'll discover your inner strength. So, make yourself strong, motivate yourself daily, and most importantly, enjoy your college life. This time will never come back, and it's a chapter of your life that will shape who you are for years to come. Be proud of your journey, no matter how difficult it may seem, because every step forward is a step closer to your dreams.

'With courage to face challenges and a vision for tomorrow.'

Regards,
Aayushi

KARAN'S STORY

Dear Reader,

'Broken But Beautiful' – this phrase carries profound significance in my life, encapsulating the journey I've had and the story that has shaped me into who I am today. To me, it speaks of resilience, the beauty that emerges from pain, and the strength found in vulnerability. It reminds me that despite life's challenges and the scars they leave behind, there's a deeper, more meaningful beauty that grows through the process.

The phrase 'Broken But Beautiful' suggests that even in the face of brokenness or imperfection, one can shine with inner strength and grace. It's about the transformation that happens when we face hardship and emerge stronger, though different from before. Life is a continuous journey of healing and growth, and I've come to embrace the beauty in my scars.

I am a passionate poet and emerging writer. Through my writing, I seek to portray the struggles, hopes, and dreams of those often unheard. Being part of a marginalised community myself and having migrated to the city of Mumbai with my family in search of better education and opportunities, I draw deeply from my own experiences when I write.

Here are some experiences of mine that have shaped me:

1. I am a UPSC CSE Failed Aspirant:

The Civil Services Examination demands dedication, perseverance, and endless hours of preparation. Three failed attempts took an immense toll on my confidence and spirit. With every setback, I questioned my worth, my abilities, and my future. However, through each failure, I also discovered my resilience. Though I felt broken, these failures taught me patience, persistence, and a deeper understanding of my strengths and limitations. My journey is far from over, and I've learned that sometimes, the most beautiful transformations happen through failure.

2. **Breakup:**

Heartbreak has a way of breaking us in ways we don't expect. My four-year relationship ended, leaving me emotionally devastated. It wasn't just the end of a relationship but the shattering of shared dreams, trust, and love. The pain was raw and overwhelming, but through the process of healing, I learned that it's possible to grow even through the cracks. The breakup forced me to face my vulnerabilities and to rebuild myself, piece by piece. While it left me broken, it also taught me self-love, resilience and the realisation that beauty can be found even in the most painful chapters of life.

3. **Pain is the Foundation of Art and Artists**

Through my personal struggles, I've come to realise that pain often serves as a powerful catalyst for creativity and self expression. Whether it is the pain of failing multiple times or the heartbreak of losing someone you loved, these experiences stir something deep within us. They push us to express what cannot be said with mere words. Pain, in its rawest form, is a source of artistic inspiration, allowing us to channel our emotions into something that resonates with others.

For me, the hardships I've endured have fuelled my desire to express myself – whether through writing, reflection, or simply the way I carry myself. Pain has a unique way of unlocking a deeper understanding of life and the world around us. Many artists create their most impactful work not in moments of joy, but from the depths of their sorrow. I now understand that the beauty of art is not always in perfection, but in the honest portrayal of human experience, no matter how broken or fragile it may seem.

In my journey of embracing brokenness and finding beauty in it, I wrote this poem as a reminder to myself, and anyone who may feel lost, that it's time to rise from the ashes

It's Time To....

It's time to fly; don't lie down to cry
Don't be shy to fly, don't ask, 'why to try?'
Be bold, don't give in to tears,
Don't let your dreams be held back by fears.

It's time to prove that you are brave,
Don't be afraid; you are not a slave,
Don't look behind and stumble and fall,
Be hungry, for you have a right to take it all.

It's time to rock the stage,
Don't be nervous it's a not a cage,
The past is gone, live in the present,
Your bright future is coming,
So, my friend, please turn the page.

This poem encapsulates everything I have learned about life: that even when we feel broken, even when life is hard, there is a beauty in perseverance, in moving forward, and in finding the courage to keep trying. It's time to embrace who I am, broken yet beautiful, and to take the next step, no matter how challenging the path ahead may seem.

Regards,
Karan

MOHIT'S STORY

Dear Reader,

I am 16 years old. I am a science student in the 11th standard at Elphinstone College, Mumbai. Despite my family's financial challenges, I am deeply grateful for what I have. Living in Mumbai, a city known for its high cost of living, owning our own house is a significant relief as it saves us from the burden of paying rent.

I come from a joint family, which I consider to be the greatest blessing in my life. Growing up in a joint family has taught me invaluable lessons about life, unity, and support. My family has always been there for me, providing unwavering support at every turn, and I am incredibly thankful for that.

When it comes to my goals, I don't have a specific career path in mind yet. My primary aim right now is to make my family financially stable. This goal drives me to work hard and stay focused on my studies. One important lesson I've learned in life is to believe in God, as He has a plan for everyone. This belief has guided me through many challenges and led me to discover the Udaan India Foundation, which has played a crucial role in my personal development.

Let me share a recent experience that highlights the importance of faith and perseverance. I chose science as my field of study but soon realised that I didn't enjoy biology. I wanted to replace it with a bifocal subject, but the cost was around ₹30,000, which was too expensive for my family. Fortunately, I found out about Elphinstone College, the only government college in Mumbai for science. Trusting in God's plan, I applied and was thrilled to get electronics instead of biology on the second list. This experience reinforced my belief that everything happens for a reason and that trusting in God's plan can lead to favourable outcomes.

In summary, my journey so far has been one of resilience, faith, and gratitude. I am determined to work hard and achieve financial stability for my family while staying true to the values and lessons I've learned along the way. I believe that with faith, perseverance, and the support of my loved ones, I can overcome any obstacle and achieve my goals.

Regards

Mohit

Monika's Story

Dear Reader,

My real journey started when I completed 10th standard. Till then, I had been studying in Hindi medium, and in 10th standard, I also got a good score. However, when I got admission into college, my difficulties started. I wasn't very good at English, and during the 11th standard, I suddenly had to struggle a bit. My family was supportive – I helped my sister with housework, and my sister and mother helped me in turn. My 11th and 12th standards went well.

Then, when my NEET exams were about to begin, my father was very unwell. Our condition at home worsened a lot. Financially and emotionally, we were very connected to our father. Because of all of this, my focus diluted and my NEET couldn't be completed.

Then, problems at home started when the college admissions process began. We three sisters faced a lot of financial problems and our mother had to pay our fees from the small savings she had.

My father was ill for a whole year, and there was no source of money in the house. When we started searching for jobs, my mother explained to us, 'No, you children will not work right now because you have to work your whole life. So, take the time to study now. Once you start getting money from the job, you will not feel like studying'. I listened to my mother and focused on my studies. After almost a year, my father's health improved, but by then, almost all our money had been spent on my father's operation and medicine, and our admission and household expenses.

I wanted to acquire other skills apart from studies, but education in basic skills like computer skills and digital marketing were quite expensive. Then I learned about Udaan from one of my friends, an NGO from which I could acquire skills apart from studies for just Rs 400, and I joined it.

It had only been a few months since I joined Udaan when the pandemic started. Due to the situation of Covid 19, it felt like one problem had not been solved yet, and another one had cropped up. Then we got laptops from Udaan, and during the pandemic, we went to our village. After getting permission from Udaan, I brought the laptop to the village and started attending online classes from there.

Then, the situation became a little normal in Mumbai, and after almost six months, our family returned to the city from the village. I started going to Udaan like before, and used to participate in everything there. The Sir there suggested that I do an internship. I did one there for four months, during which I performed well; after completing the internship, I started searching for a job, and then I had an interview and was selected. After that, I went to Gujarat for training, where I worked in a tissue-culture biotech company.

Now, I have a golden opportunity to work with those from whom I have acquired the skills. Both my younger sister and I will be working for Udaan.

When I see children like me studying, I feel proud of them for their passion. Only one thing comes to my mind: just like there is the morning after night, there comes happiness after sorrow in life.

Regards,
Monika

Aakash's Story

Dear Reader,

I was born in Mumbai. I have been a very naughty kid since childhood, always having a lot of fun. The teachers always complained to my mother, and then I would get beaten with my mother's flying sandals and comb.

When I was in class 7, there was Sports Day in my school, with games like kabaddi, running, and khoko included. I chose kabaddi, and from that day, kabaddi made a place for itself in my life. Near where I lived, Kabaddi practice used to be held in a sports field that I used to pass by daily. I told my mother that I too wanted to go for practice, but she scolded me and said that I had exams coming up and I should focus on my studies. The next evening, however, I went to practice with my sister at 7:30 pm. Mother scolded us again, but I didn't listen to her and I started practicing Kabaddi every day.

Then, in the 10th standard, Board exams entered my life and I stopped practicing for two months before the exams, thinking I would study more. When the result came out, I saw happiness on my mom and dad's faces with the 78.20% that I had scored. Then, when the selection for stream and college was going on, I wanted to take Commerce, but my family members and relatives all started saying that I should take Science because I had got such good marks. I managed to convince them that

I would study Commerce, as I wanted to also have time and energy for Kabaddi.

Our college Kabaddi team came runner-up at the district level, motivating me to keep practicing and playing. I did quite well in my 12th Boards as well, and got extra marks due to my sports achievements.

Playing a sport for me is not just about fitness or winning games. On the playing field, we are all equal, no matter where we come from, or how much money our families have. All that matters is how skilful and determined we are. I am grateful for everything I have, but want more, so that I can do my family proud, and help them.

One day, I dream of winning a gold medal for my country. It's a big dream, and I don't fully know how to get there, but I will keep trying my best, hopeful that apna time aayega!

Regards,
Aakash

Aarshi's Story

Dear Reader,

Looking back, my school and Junior College life was a roller-coaster of emotions. It was a journey of trial and error, of ups and downs, from late-night study sessions to spontaneous laughter with friends; my time in school was full of unexpected experiences that shaped me into the person I am today.

I would like to share my stories of growth, of struggle, and of self-discovery. Let's begin with my story of growth.

In the beginning, I was very shy, and I would not express my thoughts in front of my class and teachers. Even when I had the correct answer, I hesitated to speak up. I'll give you an example: when I was in 7th standard, our teacher asked us a question and no one in the class except for me knew the answer. I hesitated and could only whisper the answer to my friend, who announced the answer to the class without mentioning that I had given her the answer. It was correct, and our teacher praised her. That day, I realised that being shy was not an option. From that day, I decided that I would do my best to express myself.

When I overcame my shyness, I discovered my hidden talent of being a good student. Through this growth, I developed self-discipline and time management and learned the importance of self-confidence and self-belief. I faced failure but didn't step back, as I had the support of my family and teachers, which gave me the courage to push onward. During this journey, I also overcame self-doubt, as I realised that I could do anything that I resolved to do.

Next is my story of struggle.

Everyone faces struggles during their student life. I faced mine during Junior College. I chose to study IT, but after some time, I faced difficulty with my coursework and subjects because I was not able to understand anything. Then, I got the help of my friends and teachers, who were also very supportive and helped me to get good marks.

When I was in 11th, a close friend of mine told me we couldn't continue our friendship, and I was not able to process anything because her decision affected me deeply and messed up my mind and heart.

It took a lot of time to overcome this, so it affected my personal and academic life. This was one of the major struggles of my student life.

Then comes my story of self-discovery.

Self-discovery is one of the important parts of student life. In my journey of self-discovery, I discovered new passions and hobbies, such as writing *Shayari*s (poems), which is now one of my favourite hobbies. However, self-discovery is not only about discovering passions or hobbies; it's also about finding joy and happiness in small things like art and music.

Moreover, it is about overcoming one's fears and stepping out of one's comfort zone so one can learn new things and explore oneself. A key part of this is the journey of self-acceptance, in which a student learns to embrace one's true self and find happiness.

Regards,
Aarshi

Aaryan's Story

Hello World.

I have written this open letter so the world can know about my story and how I overcame the challenges of life. This is a story about two brothers and how their lives transformed from a prince's to a mere delivery boy's.

I would like to start with my early days when my family was so rich that I could fulfil all my needs. My Dad ran a tour and travel business and we had four cars. My mother would freely give money to those in need in our building society. We were also fully work-oriented, which drove our wealth and success in the short term. Around 7-8 years ago, this was our reality, and we had never suspected that we were living in a huge matrix.

In 2017-18, my grandfather contracted an unknown illness; our parents never told us the name because they felt we were not mature enough to understand the situation. My dad was depressed because my grandfather was in the ICU, and our business crashed. After a few months, my grandfather lost the battle for his life, despite fighting really hard.

My dad was shattered because my grandfather was his lifeline and had given him his house, job, and a happy family. Many years ago, my grandfather gave my father our house, saying that while he had lived in a slum for most of his life, my father should live in a building with his wife and children to nourish his children properly. All of this came back to my dad, and he was broken. Even during this time, though, I never saw him cry, as he continued fighting to keep it in and be an ideal father who stayed calm. One day, though, he met his friend near his office, and he broke down, crying and crying till he had shed all his tears. All his resolve broke that day, and this was a breaking point for my family. Our downfall began here and was hastened by the lockdown in which many companies had to shut down.

After a few months, out of the blue, a man came to our house and said our parents had failed to pay three consecutive EMI's of a mortgage loan of 14 lakh rupees. My brother and I were shocked that our parents had so much debt. When they came back home, we asked them about this, and what they told us shattered our minds. We did not own anything in our house, including our house itself, which was on a mortgage loan. A few days later, we found out we were in credit card debt, too. In total, the debt we had was around one crore!

My dad was already too old to get a job, and my mom couldn't get one either, so it was our responsibility to do something in this do-or-die situation.

One day, I got a call from my father's friend, who runs a medical shop. He was the first person to offer me a job. I was 14-years-old and was asked to work as a helper for 3,000 rupees per month. I happily accepted the job because no one else would have given me any work. As the days passed, it became more difficult to survive. We used to sleep late at night because we knew we had to skip breakfast and sometimes even had to skip lunch. We had hit rock bottom. Somehow, I managed to get a job as a delivery boy in another medical shop for Rs 8,000 per month, and I got a job for my brother in the same shop, too.

However, even after all of this, we could not clear the debt, so our house was sealed, and our cars were taken by the creditors.

My mother could have taken back the money from the ladies who she had helped in the lockdown, but some of them had lost their kids or had other difficulties due to which we would never recover that money.

But even after so many hurdles, we've never lost the will to work harder. I think it's in my genes never to give up. After so much struggle, I've learned many things, and the best one is that 'To solve a problem, you first have to face it'.

Through all this, I had a secret talent that I was not able to tell my parents about due to our circumstances until recently: rapping. Even in the worst times, I wrote a few rap songs. When I told them, surprisingly, my parents supported me – of course, not financially, but they gave me the moral support to create songs. For now, I still cannot really make my own songs, but one day, for sure, I'll be the greatest rapper of all time in India. For now, I just have to focus on my studies and get a good job, so my brother and I can buy a new house for our parents. I'm sure I'll be able to do that because I have a lot of courage and never-ending support from my parents.

If someone asked me what I wanted to do in my life, my priority would be purchasing a house for my parents and writing music. I'm very serious about it – I just somehow know that I'm made for the stage. I'll kill it every time I get a chance. It's just not a childish dream, but the massive faith that comes from inside that makes me feel special every time. I think you all have the same kind of energy within you, the same kind of passion within you; you just have to believe in yourself... this is my thinking, and this is my story.

Peace,

Aaryan

Aashiya's Story

Dear Readers,

I feel grateful to have parents who encouraged me to pursue education and live life on my own terms. I was born into a traditional family where girls' education was often discouraged, but my parents encouraged me to pursue education to make my life better. When I was born, my father lived in Mumbai, while my mother and I resided in our village. However, when I was four years old, we moved to Mumbai for my studies.

My father enrolled me in school in Mumbai, and my educational journey began. Everything went smoothly until I reached the 5th standard, when my father's health took a turn for the worse. He underwent numerous medical tests, and temporarily, we relocated to our village for the time of his recovery.

My mother thought that if my father lived with lots of people, he would feel better, so we went to the village, but unfortunately, some of our paternal relatives in the village were more hurtful than helpful. Instead of offering support, they discouraged my father by saying negative things. This incident taught me that no one is yours in this world except your parents. That was when I decided that I would work hard to become an independent woman and take care of my parents, so that no one would be able to say that only boys can take care of their parents.

After five to six months, my father's health improved, and we returned to Mumbai, where I resumed my studies. In 9th standard, I received the Star Student award and in 10th standard, I worked diligently and scored 88.80% in the Board exams. Because I had aimed higher, I was initially disappointed. But then, I received a laptop from Udaan as a reward for my hard work, along with a scholarship and an award and gifts from school. This recognition made me realise that setbacks often pave the way for greater opportunities.

That laptop is helping me, and it is empowering me to soar toward my goals. Today, I'm focusing on cracking the NEET medical entrance exam with dedication and perseverance. After becoming a doctor, I will show people that girls can do everything.

I extend my heartfelt gratitude to my parents, teachers, and Udaan for their unwavering guidance and support. Their faith in me has been instrumental in shaping my journey.

Thank you,
Aashiya

Aakansha's Story

Hello Everyone.

I am seventeen years old, and was born in Mumbai. I am studying in the first year of my Bachelor of Commerce degree. My father is an auto driver, and my mother is a housewife. There are seven other members in my family; I have two brothers and three sisters.

My family's condition is not good, as my father has health issues. He does not work right now. When our father became unwell, my elder brother started working, but he was not able to earn much money, so my two elder sisters' education suddenly stopped. It has been five years since my father fell ill and the shadow of that hangs over us still.

In school, when the exams were upcoming, my teacher made me stand outside because my fees were not paid. In the whole class, I was the only girl who stood outside because of my failure to pay the fees. When I was in 8th standard, the lockdown came and made our situation even more critical, so we went to our village and spent a few months there. In 10th standard, I got 72% and was admitted to a college. Then I spent two years and finished 12th standard, in which I got 65%. I was not happy with my marks, as I had wanted a higher percentage. After 10th standard, I joined Udaan. Joining Udaan made me feel very good; initially, I was afraid to talk to new people, but at Udaan I gained the courage to do this.

Udaan gives me a lot of opportunities and supports me a lot. My dream is to become a CS (Company Secretary). I took the first exam and passed it, and now I will take the second exam. If I had not had Udaan, I might not have been able to study so far. Their scholarship is what allows me to study, and I feel very lucky to get it. I have decided that I have to do something meaningful, and I will support Udaan in the future. One day, I will realise my dreams – not just for me, but to give something back to my family. One day, I will have my own EV car, in which I will take them for a drive.

Thank You,
Aakansha

Aman's Story

Dear Reader,

I was born in a small village in Uttar Pradesh. My parents, driven by the dream of giving me a better education, made the difficult decision to leave our village and move to Mumbai. It wasn't an easy transition. Many told us that we wouldn't survive city life and that we should return to the village. But my parents were determined.

When the time came for my school admission, we faced our first major hurdle. I had completed junior KG in the village, and the school wasn't eager to accept me as I hadn't completed junior KG from a city school. My mother pleaded with them, and they agreed to let me take a test. To everyone's surprise, I passed with flying colours, earning my spot.

As a student, I worked hard but remained average. While there were moments of success, overall, I was just one among many. To add to this, I had no friends. Whenever I thought I had found a friend, they would eventually start bullying me or making fun of me, as I came from such a different background. After a while, I stopped trying to make friends altogether.

Things took a turn during my 10th standard when the lockdown hit, and I passed without giving any exams. Though academically, I wasn't at the top, life outside school wasn't easy either. I was often bullied, and my mother kept me indoors, aware that the environment wasn't the best for me.

Despite my introverted nature, I dreamt big. After completing school, I faced another crossroad: Science or Commerce, which stream to take for higher studies. Initially, I wanted to pursue commerce, with dreams of becoming an IAS officer. But on the advice of others, I reluctantly chose science. Despite my efforts, I couldn't shine in that field and ended up with a 52.33% in my 12th class exams. That was the moment I truly understood life.

My father, an auto driver, once told me not to disclose his profession to my friends, fearing they wouldn't respect me. That hurt deeply. It made me realise that the world often judges us based on status, not character. From that day onward, I resolved to become a businessman and make my mark.

After much research, I discovered my true passion: Data Science. I enrolled in college and, for the first time, felt completely in control of my destiny. My hard work paid off, scoring a 9.5 CGPA in the first semester and a perfect 10 in the second. My parents were proud, and I felt like I was finally on the right path.

It was during college that I finally found a true friend, Sumit. He became my best friend, and today, he works with me in my business. I was fortunate to join the Udaan India Foundation, where I not only received valuable lessons and mentorship but was also awarded with a scholarship that covered my entire second-year fees. Udaan has been instrumental in supporting my journey, not only through education but also by helping me with ideas and guidance for my T-shirt business.

Around the same time, I stumbled upon a reel on Instagram about friends starting their own businesses. That sparked an idea: Why not start my own? And so my T-shirt printing business, was born. Despite the competition, I'm determined to make it thrive.

Today, I'm not the shy, bullied kid I once was. I've grown mentally and physically stronger, joining the gym and embracing a life of travel and adventure. My parents trust me, and I trust myself to keep pushing boundaries. As I continue this journey, one thing remains clear: I'm always striving to become the best version of myself. I'm living proof that growth is constant and success is earned, one step at a time.

Regards,
Aman

Aniket's Story

Hello All,

There are five members in my family, including myself. My father is an auto rickshaw driver, my mother is a housewife, my sister is in the Mumbai police, and my brother has a tours and travel business.

Since childhood, I have wanted to become a wealthy person, and one of my teachers suggested that I become an engineer to have a good career. Thus, I decided to become an engineer to have a better career, gain experience, and start my own business.

I worked hard in 10th grade to secure admission to a good diploma engineering college, and I was able to achieve that, thanks to the Udaan and Udaan alumni teams' support.

However, I considered cancelling my admission in the first month itself because the college environment was totally new for me, and I had studied in a vernacular medium before. The first one or two months were very difficult, but I didn't give up and decided to go with the flow and cope with the situation. Attending a spoken English programme for beginners after my 10th examination helped me a lot. In this programme, I learned various things, such as grammar and sentence formation.

After graduating from college, I was ready to work. However, I found cracking interviews very difficult. Fortunately, Udaan provided the Let's Write and Let's Talk programme, which helped me learn how to give interviews and secure a job. In this programme, they taught us everything from interview preparation to formal mail writing, which really helped me in my corporate life.

At work, every day, I come across many problems and challenges, but I understand and accept that life itself is a challenge, so I deal with all challenges well.

Also, I have some anger issues. I have successfully managed them to a good extent and am still working on them, as I believe that we need to face any challenge calmly and patiently and work towards a solution rather than wasting time.

Yours,

Aniket

Ankit's Story

Dear Reader,

I was just another teenager, cruising through life, until the lockdown hit after 10th grade. The world outside had come to a standstill, but my academic journey was supposed to keep moving – easier said than done. Distractions were everywhere, and studying online seemed impossible. I struggled to focus, and my 12th-grade results suffered. The pressure to clear JEE mounted, but I wasn't prepared. I tried again the next year but still couldn't crack it. Exhaustion set in.

As I considered college admissions, I felt overwhelmed. BTech programmes seemed daunting, with eight hours of classes, plus three hours of daily travel. Would I have time for anything else? That's when I stumbled upon online degrees. Arvind Arora sir's YouTube channel opened my eyes to this alternative. I discovered IIT Madras's distance learning programme in Electronic Systems. It seemed too good to be true.

With renewed determination, I studied for a month and cleared the entrance exam. I had done it! Now, I'm pursuing my passion for learning through distance education. Now that I have enough time, I look forward to Udaan's resources to develop soft skills and get some basic knowledge in different courses. I've discovered a new love for learning. Looking back, I realise that distractions can be opportunities in disguise, and failure is not the end but a chance to reassess and find alternative paths.

My journey has taught me valuable lessons. I've learnt to embrace uncertainty and explore alternative paths. Failure is a stepping stone to growth, and self-directed learning can unlock new opportunities. I've also learned not to be afraid to take the road less travelled and that every setback is an opportunity for a comeback. I've come to cherish the journey, not just the destination. My story is a reminder that life's twists and turns can lead to incredible discoveries.

Regards,
Ankit

Santoshi's Story

Dear Reader,

Today, it has been 20 years since I joined Udaan and I am proud that I am the first student of Udaan. Let me tell you how my 20 years old story started.

I had never thought that I would ever be able to go to school. Both my parents worked and I used to play with my friends at home. We used to live in a colony nearby. One day, three Didis came and all of them talked to our family and took us to Udaan from that colony. On 16th August 2004, we went to Udaan for the first time and I started my studies. Every day Didi used to tell us and teach us something new. Whenever Didi used to tell us something, I used to think that I would also become like Didi and my dream was to become a teacher. After a few days, I was admitted to the school and I was able to see the school for the first time and go there. Because of Udaan, my experience of that school was very amazing. For me, it was no less than a dream but Udaan is my first school where I learnt everything. When I told my dream to Didi, she helped me a lot in fulfilling my dream.

Many children have to struggle a lot to fulfil them, but I did not have to because I had Udaan and Didi with me. Today, if there was no Udaan, I would never have been able to go to school or study. All these things became possible because of Udaan and today I have become a teacher. I have fulfilled my dream. Just like I fulfilled my dream, in the same way Udaan is helping many children like me fulfil their dreams by teaching them.

Hum Honge Kamyaab (We will overcome) is the Udaan school song where we all together achieve success.

I consider myself very lucky because I got a family like Udaan, we are Udaan and we are Udaan.

Think big, dream big, believe big and the result will be big, this is the moto of Udaan.

Thanks!
Santoshi

Ankita's Story

Dear Reader,

I am a mechanical engineer, working in a MNC. This story started when I was born. No one was happy at home as I was the second daughter born in the house, after my sister. My mom struggled a lot as my grandmother did not like me at all, so my mom had to take care of me alone along with doing all the household work. Sometimes, I would cry and no one would pay attention. Mummy was always upset and my grandparents never appreciated me.

I started schooling in Hindi medium with my four brothers. Our financial condition was not that good. We were just enduring it, living a normal life, and then one day, my father's friend told us about the Udaan India Foundation, and we joined it. My brother told me that there would be a test for admission, which I was confident of passing as I was good in studies. I was shocked when my brother told me that I had failed the test.

That day, I cried a lot. I had lost my confidence. However, my brother told me that there would be a re-test, so I gave it, and, this time, I passed. In class 5, I joined Udaan, and soon it became like another family for us. I was always very excited to go to the Udaan centre. There used to be an assembly every day and then I had to study. I would give all the monthly tests and participate in all the events held for festivals. After joining Udaan, my confidence also increased. Suddenly, it was as if

I could stand in front of a hundred people and speak. While doing this, the day came when it was time for me to leave Udaan because my school timings changed, and I came to 9th standard.

Now, my focus was on 10th because I wanted to break the record for Udaan students, which was 94%. For two years, I only studied. I studied day and night, and after many long months, my exams at last happened. Now, it was time to rejoin Udaan's youth programme, where I started the English-speaking course (Yuva). Those holidays went by well with my friends, but I didn't understand the course at all.

All this time, I had been waiting for the day of the results, and finally it came. I got 90.4%. I had not broken Udaan's record, but I was the first child in my family to get a score above 90%. After this good result, I started thinking more about what I would do next. I was already sure that I would be an engineer, and this was when I decided that I would pursue a diploma in mechanical engineering.

I remember, when I said this at home, my parents said that mechanical engineering is not for girls. My Didi at Udaan, who was close to me, advised me to first complete 11th and 12th standard to build understanding and then go for engineering by giving the JEE or CET, but I was adamant. I was insistent on doing diploma, and I took admission. My Didi then supported me, helping me a lot in my studies and making my mother and father understand that girls can do everything. My performance vindicated her – I completed my diploma and left the college with a good placement.

Now was the time to leave college and enter the corporate sector, independent of my family, teachers, and everyone else, but something felt incomplete. Our financial condition was still not good, so I had to support my family and could not complete my degree. Then, I decided to get a job to complete my degree, while financially supporting my family. I completed my engineering as well, while working at an office.

Today, I am the first girl in my entire village to become an Engineer. I have made my mother, father, Udaan and my Udaan Didi feel proud.

Regards,
Ankita

PREETI'S STORY

Dear Reader,

I live in Sangharsh Nagar, Chandivali, Mumbai. I am 15 years old. My father is a carpenter, and my mother is a housewife. I have three older sisters and one younger brother. My mother and sister work hard to support our family, which is middle-class.

My dream is to become a Chartered Accountant. People think that girls can't do anything, and I want to prove them wrong through my journey

I aspire to visit Kedarnath first, with my family and do some social work with NGOs because many children are denied education due to financial problems. I want to help them because every child has the right to education.

My journey of fifteen years has been full of nervousness, fear, happiness, sadness, and challenges. It is difficult to describe it in a few lines. In the 1st standard, I got admission to a government school. I was very bad in studies till the 3rd standard, as I did not appreciate the importance of studies. Then, I joined the NGO Udaan India Foundation.

My Didi there scolded me because I would not study, and complained to my mother. I was afraid, especially when my sister started teaching me at home, armed with a stick. But that changed everything – it was the first and last complaint about me that went home. Over the years, I studied diligently. When the time of my Boards came, there was a family issue that made me even more tense, but I still gave my best and got 92% in SSC Board, coming first in my school. My teachers and family were proud of me, and I got the Student of the Year and the All-Rounder award. I also got second prize in a poem competition and many other certificates and medals at school and at Udaan, which boosted my confidence. Now, I am in 11th standard at SK Somaiya college.

During COVID, we all had many problems, but Udaan helped me and my family by distributing phones and rations. I am very proud to be an alumnus of Udaan. When I look back, I see that half of my problems dissipated when I entered Udaan. Udaan helped me emotionally and mentally. When I felt that I couldn't do anything, my family and Udaan encouraged me and reminded me that I could achieve anything in my life. A friend of mine also stood by me and guided me in such times.

What I have learned, through the guidance of others and my own experiences, is that if you are born poor, it is not your fault, but if you die poor, that will be your fault because if you work hard to achieve your goals you can be so powerful.

Yours lovingly,
Preeti

PRITI'S STORY

Dear Reader,

I was born into a middle-class family in the heart of Uttar Pradesh. From the moment I entered this world, my story has been marked by a mix of emotions.

My paternal grandparents were not pleased with my birth, simply because I was a girl. They held on to the old belief that a boy child was more valuable. But to my parents, I was a precious gift. I was their first child, and for them, I was the light of their lives. My maternal grandparents were also overjoyed. They celebrated my birth with a grand party and followed all the traditional rituals.

After 6-8 months, I was diagnosed with pneumonia. My maternal grandfather said to the doctor, 'Dr Saheb, please take my whole bag of money, but cure my daughter'. I fought against pneumonia and got well soon.

Growing up as the eldest of four siblings, I became a protective older sister to my three younger brothers. Together, we shared many joys and struggles, but life was about to take us on a big journey. When I was around 10 years old, my family made a life-changing decision to move to Mumbai. The shift was hard for all of us, but my parents believed that the city would offer better educational opportunities. Despite the financial strain, they enrolled me in an English-medium school, determined to give me the best education possible. They knew education was the key to my future, and my mother was especially dedicated to my studies. She never let any hurdle stop me from reaching my potential. When I was in 7th standard, I was diagnosed with tuberculosis (TB). After a six-month treatment, I overcame TB. Throughout this, my mother had faith in me, which kept me strong.

In fact, she had so much faith in me that she brought a box of sweets home a day before the results of high school were even out, saying, 'My girl will make us proud; I know it'. And she was right. I scored 89.60% in high school and was the topper of my school. I will never forget the pride in my parent's eyes, the happiness of my teachers, and the excitement I felt at that moment.

Due to my high school success, I got admission to S.K. Somaiya College, one of the most reputed colleges in Mumbai. I chose the science stream, studying Physics, Chemistry, Mathematics, and Biology. Though my results in junior college weren't as high as I had hoped – I scored 67.83% – I never lost sight of the bigger picture.

My father had always dreamt of seeing me become a doctor. His dream was born out of personal loss; my grandfather had passed away due to the unavailability of doctors in our village when he needed medical attention the most. But the path to becoming a doctor wasn't easy. With my father's dream as my motivation, I set my sights on preparing for the National Eligibility Cum Entrance Test (NEET), the entrance exam for medical colleges. However, there was one big hurdle – money. We couldn't afford the expensive coaching classes that were necessary for NEET preparation.

During this challenging time, I came across an NGO called Udaan India Foundation. For me, the Udaan India Foundation wasn't just an organisation. it was family, love, and support in its truest form. Through Udaan, I met Malkawa Didi, one of the most inspiring people I've met. She introduced me to Udaan's programmes, and from there, my life started to change. She also introduced me to a Didi, who has been my guiding light. This Didi believed in me from the start. She saw potential in me even when I doubted myself. With her support, I decided to take a drop year and fully focus on preparing for NEET.

She arranged for me to attend coaching classes and even paid all the fees. Moreover, she gave me a laptop, which became my lifeline for studying. 'You are not alone in this journey', she said. 'We're here with you, every step of the way'. This gave me hope for my future. During my preparation, my mother fell ill and was hospitalised, so I had to manage my studies and support her, such as by doing household chores.

When I first joined Udaan, I enrolled in English Speaking classes and learned computer skills from Shailesh and Anurag Bhaiya. With the guidance of Sushree Didi, I mastered email writing, a skill I never knew I would enjoy so much. One of the most memorable moments of my time with Udaan was joining a programme called 'Let's Talk'. Through this programme, I had the opportunity to meet and interact with Dr Annoottam Ghosh Sir, the trustee of Udaan. The experience gave me newfound confidence, and for the first time, I began to believe in my own voice and abilities. Now, he is my mentor as well.

Through Udaan, I also got a one-month internship at Abbott, a world-renowned healthcare Company. I worked as a STEM intern in the Abbott Diabetes Care Department. During this internship, I worked on a project called Understanding and Winning in Government e-Marketplace. The opportunity to visit pharmacy channels, work on I&D, and network with new people from around the APAC region was amazing, and I learned, grew, and had so much fun. This has given me great insights into the industry and has motivated me, which will definitely help me in my future endeavours.

In 2023, I cleared the NEET exam. While I could have pursued MBBS, my heart had led me toward a slightly different path – Physiotherapy. I realised that through physiotherapy, I could still serve people, helping them heal and recover while being part of the medical field. Once again, my Udaan Didi was there to help me, supporting me by paying my fees for the Bachelor of Physiotherapy (BPTh) programme.

As I write this in 2024, I am currently in my first year of BPTh. Every day I walk into that college, I remind myself that I am one step closer to achieving not just my dream but my father's dream. 'You will be the first doctor in the family', he always says. And soon, I will be.

My journey has been filled with challenges but also with love, support, and guidance from incredible people like my parents and the Udaan India Foundation, especially my Didi and Ghosh Sir. I want to give back to the community that shaped me, to bring hope and healing to those who need it the most – just like Udaan and my Didi did for me. They have taught me that when you believe in yourself and when others believe in you, too, no obstacle is too great.

I know there are still more hurdles to cross, but I am ready for them.

As I look to the future, I carry with me the lessons from my past: that with hard work, dedication, and the right support, dreams – no matter how big – are always within reach.

And I'm just getting started.

Yours,

Priti

Priyanka's Story

Dear Reader,

While doing my BMS degree, I found myself searching for meaningful ways to start my career. In 2022, I came across the Udaan India Foundation, a place that seemed perfect for my learning. My first programme at Udaan was Basic Literacy, where I was fortunate to learn from Priya Ma'am, one of my favourite teachers. She didn't just teach content; she inspired me with her passion and dedication to make a difference. It was a great way to begin my journey.

I interned at Udaan for six months, and during that time, I learned so much more than I ever imagined. It wasn't just about helping kids learn but also about understanding their struggles and offering them a sense of hope. The experience made me realise how powerful education can be in shaping lives, and I'm incredibly grateful to Udaan for giving me the opportunity to be part of something so impactful. Those six months were truly a turning point for me, and I carry the lessons I learned there daily.

Equipped with new skills, I did an internship after this. However, I then went through a challenging phase. I wasn't doing anything work-related for four months, because I was faced with uncertainty, which was difficult to navigate. I didn't know what direction to take next, which sometimes felt frustrating. But during this time, I found something valuable: spending time with my family. There are five of us, and the time I spent with them during those months was precious. Their constant support, understanding, and encouragement gave me the strength to keep going. Looking back, I see that period as a time of personal growth, where I learned the importance of patience and family.

Eventually, things took a positive turn when I got an opportunity to intern at General Mills in the supply chain team, thanks to my experience at Udaan. The corporate world was a whole new experience, but I was eager to learn and challenge myself. I was rewarded with a job opportunity at General Mills. Working there has been an eye-opener in many ways. I've gained insights into how supply chains operate and how different pieces come together to make things run smoothly. Every day, I'm learning new skills that I know will be valuable as I move forward in my career.

While work keeps me busy, I've always made sure to stay connected with passions outside of my professional life. One of my greatest joys is traveling and spending time in nature. There's something about being outdoors that refreshes and energises me. I've travelled to several places, but one of my favourite experiences was trekking at Tungeshwar. It was a thrilling experience, walking through the trails and being surrounded by nature's beauty. Trekking gives me a sense of peace and adventure, and I try to make time for it whenever I can.

Looking ahead, I know there's still so much to explore, both in my career and in life. I want to continue pushing myself, learning new things, and growing as a person. Whether it's through my work or my love for travel, I believe every experience teaches us something valuable. I'm excited to see where the future takes me and am always ready for new challenges and opportunities that come my way.

Regards,
Priyanka

Badri

Hello, Dear Readers,

I come from Odisha – a place renowned for its warm people and rich cultural heritage.

Born into a loving middle-class family, I was raised amidst the vibrant traditions and values that define this beautiful region. I am currently living in Mumbai, the 'city of dreams'. Mumbai, with its blend of chaos and charm, has taught me many valuable lessons on my journey of discovery, which I am excited to share with you all.

I have always been an ambitious child, driven by aspirations to be like my father. Decades ago, everything was good in the family, thanks largely to the success of my grandfather's business. One day, he was travelling back home from the *Tirth Yatra* with his wife and three children when he got to know that his business had gone bankrupt. He had handed over the business to his two most-trusted friends while he was away, but they took all the money he had accumulated over the years.

That was his darkest day, and from there, things only got worse. The family debt skyrocketed, and my grandfather was bedridden by depression. My uncle worked to support the family, and my father was forced to begin working in class ten, at a printing press. After that, striving for opportunities, he used the money from his work at a mill to move to Bahrain, where he lived for over ten years. His toil there paid off; upon his return to Mumbai, he could relieve my family of all our debt and take a home in Mumbai. His story inspired me to work for what I wanted.

My father wished for me to become an IAS officer, an old dream of his, but my interest lay in finance. When this difference arose, instead of imposing his wishes on me, he pushed me on and encouraged me to pursue my own ambitions. I dreamt of becoming a CFA and starting something of my own. The study required was long and hard at times, but my father's story drove me, kindling an insatiable hunger that I know will never be satisfied till I achieve my goal. This attitude helped me to become a good student and to score well in both SSC and HSC in the commerce field, with 82% and 91%, respectively.

I am ready to face all the upcoming challenges and give my best to fulfil my dreams. My experiences have taught me something I would love to convey to you: be passionate about your goals, and you can achieve everything you want. God has given you one chance to you to prove your worth, so make it count.

Warm regards,
Badri

ARCHANA'S STORY

Hello,

My dream is to become a doctor. If I had to give the essence of my life in one word, I would choose the word 'opportunity'. This is because, from the beginning to the end, everything in life is like an opportunity. We should just have the right perspective to see the opportunities. The chance to be born on this earth is our first and biggest opportunity. Then, at every age, every special moment, everything that gives us happiness, is an opportunity. Life keeps giving us opportunities to prove ourselves at school, at home, and everywhere else, all the time – opportunities to prove and improve ourselves.

My life has also been full of opportunities, and since childhood I have naturally taken every opportunity without thinking, which has helped me develop myself. I have learned a lot from my friends, family members and people around me. For instance, I learned from my friends that one should not have false expectations and believe in others without reason. I learned from my family that the farther you advance on the path of life, the more alone you will become, so don't fear the path of life. Rather, walk on it happily because many paths are open for the one who is alone. However, my family has also taught me not to break my ties with the earth because that is when pride sets in, bringing its own set of problems and making us distant from ourselves.

In the eyes of my family members, I have been smart since childhood. Actually, everybody has always respected me a lot because I don't have a brother. My father, in particular, has respected me and always praises me in front of others, saying that I have been very active since childhood and am smart in everything. I used to get As in school mostly, and whenever my parents would go to school for the Parent Teacher Meetings, my teachers would never complain, telling them that I was very good at studies. No one believed I would ever get low marks, but I did in 5th standard.

My teachers also complained about me and my lack of focus. I didn't know why, but I felt very bad and started comparing myself with everyone. I started having so much self-doubt that I was not even able to believe the answers I had written. I even stopped trusting my notes, so I would take notes from all the other students. When checking answers, I would cross-check with their work, believing they must be doing it better than I was. Eventually, though, I understood that one should believe in oneself, and this realisation helped me become more independent and confident.

Soon, I had taken my previously held place in the eyes of my family. When my sisters reached 10th standard, my father would get very animated, motivating them to study well. But when I came in 10th, I thought that whatever happens, father will be happy, I have to get so many marks and I gave my best. After the completion of 9th but before school started, I came to know that I had a lump in my breast. I got scared, wondering why this was happening to me.

When my operation took place, my doctor treated me very well, and I felt that I want to become a doctor, inspired by him. I started studying very hard, and gave it my best. I was very hopeful that at least papa would say something nice but he said nothing, and after one year he asked how much I had scored in 10th, and he hardly reacted, saying I would do better next time. In 12th as well, he hardly reacted to my results, and I was disheartened for a while, but resolved that I would make him proud one day. By becoming a doctor, I can make him proud of being a doctor's father because 10th or 12th results are not remembered for long but the title of 'doctor' will remain with my name always.

Regards

Archana

ARJUN'S STORY

Dear Reader,

I am a BSc IT graduate, currently working as a Data Analyst.

We are a family of five brothers and three sisters. My parents used to work at construction sites. Born and brought up in the slums of Hiranandani, Powai, I would play and spend my childhood with other children of my age.

I want to go to all the places I can; I want to see and visit the whole of India and experience the joy of meeting people, making better communities, learning, and motivating others! My dream was to join the armed forces, but I couldn't due to the age limit. But I don't regret not being part of it; at least I could appear for the SSB interview because I had confidence in myself, confidence that Udaan had built in me. Although I couldn't clear the interview, it taught me many other lessons – to not give up and to always be hard-working and perseverant.

I wanted to go to school but couldn't as my mama and papa wouldn't get time off work. I still remember playing with my friends when my Udaan Didi suddenly came there to ask about our whereabouts. She took us along with our parents' permission. This was the turning point of my life. I was among the first batch of students of Udaan – among the very first saplings sowed by Udaan to make lives better and greener in a barren land.

We got proper coaching, food, and all the resources that a child pursuing education should get and the life skills that keep one going and growing. Didi saw the spark in me and some other children and took us to school, got us enrolled there, and my education began. I had never thought I would get the chance to go to an English medium school and interact with teachers from abroad, but Udaan made that possible. It left no stone unturned in its effort to bring the best to us. We would have extra classes for English grammar, life skills, and maths every day before school, taken by Julia Ma'am, an integral part of my childhood. I feel proud of my Udaan Didi, Julia Ma'am, Mrs Mave Didi, my parents, my siblings, Udaan, and all the teachers and selfless volunteers for everything.

They have made the world a better place to live for every child like me. Today I'm a grown-up working person, helping others grow along with me. I'm one of the many sparks created by Udaan to ignite this beautiful world fuelled by education.

Regards,

Arjun

BHUMIKA'S STORY

Hello Readers

I am in my second year of management studies, and I am 18 years old.

I am the youngest at home. I have three siblings, and they all are older than me. When I was born, I already had two sisters. My uncles and aunts tried to force my mom to exchange me with a boy. My mom stood firm and didn't let them sway her, so I am really proud of her. Now, my family is proud of me because, in my entire family, no one has scored the percentage that I have scored. I used to be the topper of my class and the favourite student of my schoolteachers.

I was born and raised in a slum area. Those were the best days of my life. I have many memories there, how my siblings and I used to go to school together, eat together, and enjoy. I've created many memories there, but that was not the end of my story. My family and I shifted from one place to another. At first, my father was the only one who was earning, but then, during COVID, because of Udaan, my brother got a job at General Mills. He bought a house for our family, which was the best moment for us.

At the same time, my father got a notice that we had to vacate the house we were living in then, but we were happy because we had our own home. Life there, however, wasn't very good. Our environment was unfamiliar, our schedule was changed, and many of us were falling sick. We wanted to stay there as it was our home, but there were many issues, like water, air, and noise pollution. My brother then decided to buy us a new house in another building, and it was his best decision. Now, our family is beautiful and happy.

We may have our own house, but my responsibility is to do more in life and give my family whatever they want so that they can fully transition from having nothing to having everything.

That was my story. Hope you guys liked it.

Regards,
Bhumika

ARUP'S STORY

Hello Everyone,

I am an 18-year-old boy filled with the dreams of achievements and success that everyone has. I come from a middle-class Bengali family. For my family, happiness is the most important thing. I have just completed my schooling and am dreaming of a career in the aviation industry, but this path has not been without challenges.

The biggest challenge I faced was when I was in my 12th standard. It was November, and my birthday was around the corner – I was so excited! Suddenly, a couple of weeks before my birthday, I suddenly started feeling dizzy and irritable. My parents took me to a child specialist, who gave me some medicines, putting my condition down to normal teenage anxieties.

Now December started, and my pre-Board exams were upon me. I was fairly confident, other than Math, which is a subject I intensely disliked, and hoped I'd somehow score above 50 or something. I was done with my second pre-Board exam when I came home, barely in my senses. My mother thought I was tired and asked me to sleep. When she came to wake me up after four hours, she was shocked as I was burning with fever. My father, mother, and aunt rushed me to the government hospital, where they recommended an X-ray.

After my X-ray arrived, the doctor said that I might have tuberculosis. I remember the shock on my parents' faces. They were so dazed that when my father's wallet was stolen on the way back from the hospital, he didn't even notice.

It was then that I first realised what my parents would be going through. They were worried about my health and about whether I would recover at all. I also began thinking of the huge financial burden it would be on my family. What would happen if I couldn't even appear for my Board exams? What lay in my future? How would I ever be able to help my parents? Perhaps for the first time, I realised that they had been responsible for me all my life, and now it was my time to grow up and also take on some responsibility. They had worked hard to give me the life and opportunities I had, and now I could not let them down.

I asked my parents not to worry on my account and that I would be strong and face whatever came my way if they were also strong. The report came back confirming tuberculosis, but instead of panicking, I took the medicines the doctor prescribed, tried to keep myself positive, and prepared for my exams. My family stood behind me every day, and despite my pain and fever, I felt that I was not alone. We were facing this together. My mother constantly cared for me, giving me nutritious food every few hours, and chasing me to take my medicines, and the rest of the family cared for me, and constantly prayed for me. I managed to beat tuberculosis, and passed my exams with 68 per cent marks. Part of me wonders how much better I could have done if I had not been ill, but largely, I am grateful I could see through those dark days.

That experience taught me many things – the importance of health above all else; the fact that family is the one support system we will always have; and finally, how we have a responsibility to stay positive no matter what comes our way and trust in the Almighty.

Regards,
Arup

Mukesh's Story

Hello,

Through my journey, I have learnt that 'changes are the truth of reality', and my journey has been sort of a rollercoaster. My first few years of schooling were wonderful, and life seemed to be a playground. Till the 6th grade, I was in a nearby Hindi medium school, and I was totally in my comfort zone, surrounded by children from a similar background, with every day filled with fun.

Then came a change that was traumatic at the time, but perhaps the best decision my parents took for me. They knew that to improve my lot in life, education was the key, and while I was too young at the time to think of such things, they wanted me to dream of a future that was better than my past.

They put me in an English medium school. I was too young to appreciate the sacrifices they were making by putting me in a more expensive school, and all I was focused on was how alien this new world was to me. I was surrounded by kids who spoke an alien language, who dressed differently, who seemed to be from a different world. I became timid and introverted and began to lose confidence. It took me a while to start to find my footing.

I joined the Udaan skill programme after finishing 10th grade. This was my first real dive into the world beyond traditional academics. Suddenly, I was learning skills that made me see the world differently. This period was a whirlwind of growth and discovery, a stark contrast to my previously sheltered life, and an experience that made me realise just how big the world was, the immense opportunities it offered, and how education and confidence could help me grab those opportunities.

College brought its own set of challenges. Adjusting to a more advanced syllabus was tough, but I managed. Just as I was getting the hang of things, the pandemic hit. I had imagined this time of my life would be a period of freedom and exploration, but instead, it brought isolation and uncertainty. I struggled with online classes and found myself glued to my phone. My mom, however, was a rock during this time. Her practical skills and guidance helped us navigate through the tough days, and I learned a lot about resilience and survival.

After navigating the storm of the pandemic, I decided to take a break from formal education to focus on myself. I pursued a digital marketing course to upskill and explore new interests. Eventually, I enrolled in a Bachelor of Management Studies (BMS) programme, hoping it would be a fulfilling experience. But reality didn't quite match my expectations, and I began to question whether a learning environment can truly shape our minds.

I'm still on this journey, embracing every twist and turn. I'm learning to accept change as a constant and am excited for the new stories and growth that lie ahead.

Yours,
Mukesh

ASHA'S STORY

Dear All

I am an overthinker and a daydreamer, and a girl who thinks that we shouldn't share our pain with others. My family is from Uttar Pradesh. I am 23 years old, and according to the customs of many families from my State, I should have had children by now. I have done interior designing, but have allowed everyone in my village to believe that for the last 3-4 years, I have been repeatedly appearing for and failing the 12th grade exams. If they got to know I have studied so much further, they would get a heart attack and would forcefully get me married.

But despite all of this, I have many dreams. My mom and dad are supportive. They are not that educated but still they never stopped me from studying. I am very fond of acting, dancing and singing. I have participated in all these many times in college. I also like story writing and storytelling and more than my hobby, if I ever get a chance to make something out of it, I will definitely take it.

As for travelling, that is every girl's dream. It's a different matter that I have not travelled even in my local region, but I would soon like to travel to different parts of India, such as Kerala. Visiting Vrindavan in Uttar Pradesh, though, is the most important for me, as Lord Krishna spent his childhood there. When it comes to foreign countries, I would love to go to places like Iceland and Paris.

If we talk about life, that keeps going with the flow. I hadn't known, though, that the flow would be so unpredictable and that life would have all these ups and downs. There are some such things in my life that I am afraid to discuss even with myself. There are some things which I have not been able to tell even my parents and perhaps I will never be able to tell them.

In my childhood, if someone would ask me what I wanted to become, I would just say 'doctor' or 'teacher' or something. But as life changed its course, things became clear, and I started to understand that life would not be so easy. I sometimes think of the contrast between my childhood, when I used to consider myself rich if I got 5 rupees, and now when I am never satisfied and am always thinking about what I could have done with more money.

When I was in class 11, I used to see my friends who had boyfriends. The whole year, they would not focus on studies and would go out wherever they wanted to, but would still get good marks. Seeing this, I would think about how some people can achieve so much with just a little effort while others lag behind even if they put their soul into something.

It was a strange situation because there were so many restrictions, dreams, and responsibilities that created confusion, and amidst all this, it felt like the time of my graduation came in no time. The biggest challenge for me was that I had to go out and meet people from far away because my mom and dad could tell me only as much as they knew, but I had to know more. So, I chose a college that was quite far away, and this was the first local train journey of my life. I did not tell my parents about this.

Once, I fell from the train and hurt myself, but I had to be strong, get up and get on with it. In that one week, I understood this that it was the best decision of my life because when I fell, no one cared much; everyone was busy with themselves, and the rest who paid attention were scolding me even when I was not at fault.

That day, I understood that there is a huge difference between learning to live alone in life and being alone. For me, challenges themselves became a means of progress. I learned from all the people I met when to lose in a war and when to win. However, I also realised my biggest shortcoming: taking things to heart very quickly.

Now, I just want to work on this shortcoming, but who knows what life is going to teach me in this chapter? The best learning for me has been that while we always think the grass is greener on the other side, I don't want to look at others' gardens; instead, I want to focus on growing a lot of flowers in my garden to make it beautiful. I want to do something that makes the people who have helped me reach here and myself proud.

Thank you

Asha

ASHISH'S STORY

Dear Reader,

Growing up in the slums of Mumbai, in a small house that barely fit the four of us, life always seemed to offer more questions than answers. My father worked long hours as an auto-rickshaw driver, and my mother cleaned houses to make ends meet. As a kid, I didn't understand the weight they carried, but I felt it – every time I saw my dad return home, exhausted, and my mother's hands, which were roughened from scrubbing floors.

In school, I had always excelled in Mathematics, but English was my constant challenge. When I entered Commerce studies, I quickly realised that the gap in my language skills was becoming a barrier. It wasn't just about passing exams; I felt powerless when I couldn't express myself confidently. Instead of giving up, I made the library my second home, devouring books to improve my English. I Joined Udaan, and there I immersed myself in a series of courses – Yuva, Teach India, Career Ready, Let's Write, Let's Talk and Advanced Excel. Each step brought new challenges and insights, slowly shaping my ability to tackle real-life problems. With every lesson, I found my confidence growing, no longer feeling overwhelmed by the obstacles before me but instead feeling ready to face them head-on.

When it was time for college, I knew that asking my parents for financial help wasn't an option. They were already stretched too thin. So, I took jobs – washing cars in the morning, delivering newspapers at dawn, and handing out pamphlets between classes. I saved every rupee, and when I finally had enough to cover my fees, it was a moment of pride I'll never forget. I wasn't just studying commerce; I was living it. It wasn't just about money but about proving to myself that I could make things happen, no matter the odds.

In March 2020, life threw another curveball. I found myself in the hospital, fighting a life-threatening condition. Those days in the hospital were some of the darkest. Recovery was long and hard, but it gave me time to reflect. I knew that I wanted to create something meaningful. That's when I launched my first business idea, which was similar to Blinkit or Zepto. Unfortunately, it didn't take off, but it wasn't the failure that bothered me. Instead, it became the motivation I needed to launch Aplepustak, a new venture that took off and gave me hope.

Aplepustak's success opened doors. Together, my friend and I entered business competitions like Skill-a-thon and Eureka by IIT Bombay, showcasing our ideas and seeing early success. Each time we presented our ideas, I felt like I was reclaiming the years of struggle and turning them into something that mattered. Today, I carry those lessons forward – resilience, adaptation, and the belief that failure is never the end, only a stepping stone. But success in the market didn't last. The challenges we faced started piling up, and despite our best efforts, we were not ready for the crises that came our way. Eventually, we made the difficult decision to shut down Aplepustak. It wasn't easy, but it was the only choice we had if we wanted to move forward.

After the end of Aplepustak, I knew I had to pivot. I began preparing for the CFA (Chartered Financial Analyst) exam. This opened doors I hadn't imagined. I immersed myself in the world of finance, gaining expertise in investment markets, economics, and business analytics. I even began investing in micro-businesses, using my experience to guide me. The success I've found in this field is only the beginning.

Looking back, the journey has been long and hard, but I'm still just getting started. When I was at my lowest, people left me. When I needed them most, I found myself alone, struggling to climb a mountain that seemed too high. But I believe that if I can reach the top on my own, the view will be worth every moment of hardship.

That's my story, and it's still being written.

Yours,
Ashish

Bhumi's Story

Dear Reader,

Earlier, my life was a little strange – there were problems, but I could not understand what the real issue was. Still, there was a strange happiness, maybe because life was simple in the village, so it felt like everything was fine. But when I came to Mumbai, things started changing. Every day, there were new problems and struggles. It seemed that this city was not for me, and it would be better to go back to the village to finish my studies. But nothing like this could happen, so I spent my 8th, 9th and 10th standards here in Mumbai.

Tenth standard was the most challenging time for me. Due to family problems, giving Board Exams had become very tough. I did not feel like studying at all. Sometimes, I felt like giving up my life and giving up everything.

It had been decided that I would return to the village after the 10th standard, but my parents told me first to join computer classes in Udaan India. I was not at all interested, but I had to agree. When I attended it on the first day, though, I liked it. Slowly, one month passed, and I started getting to know a lot of people. Many people already knew me because my sister was also studying there.

Once, a cricket match was organised at Udaan, but it was only for the boys. We girls told Ma'am that we also wanted to play, so she allowed us. My first match went quite well and the second match even better. I also got the Woman of the Match prize. Then, a few days later, it was my birthday, and we celebrated it very well. After that day, whenever there was any event, my name was the first to be mentioned. This is where the changes started in my life.

In the meantime, Mummy's health became very bad, due to which I could not go to class for a week. One day, when I went to class, I shared all my problems with a Didi at Udaan who was very close to me. She said a simple thing to me, 'Why are you getting tensed? Udaan is there for you – this is your second family'. This made me feel better, and from then on, I decided that whatever happened, I would always say yes to any event or work related to Udaan.

Now, Udaan is not just a class for me – it has actually become my second family. I now see the people there as my people. I feel that Udaan is the best foundation in the world, which not only teaches studies but also teaches a new way of living life. It is like a family where everyone has their own importance.

Now, I have only one goal – to do something big in life and reach my destination. When I fulfil my dreams, I will help other children reach their destination. I know that the real path of my life starts from here, and I will never look back. No matter how many problems come in life, there is always a solution, and one should never give up.

Regards,
Bhumi

Chanda's Story

Dear Reader,

My journey started in 2009 when I joined a local corporation school in class one. Initially, I was very weak in studies, but since the government had passed a law that said no student could be failed till 8th standard, I passed from the first to the 3rd standard. When I came to the 3rd standard, I noticed that the teachers behaved very nicely with students who studied well, addressing their doubts and focusing primarily on them. As I was not a good student, they ignored me and shouted at me. When I noticed this, I decided I had to change myself.

This was when I joined Udaan – because I thought my friends were good at studies just because they had joined Udaan. After admission there, I tried to improve my academics slowly. After one or two years, I became the topper of my class. My teachers started giving me the same attention that they used to give others, and every teacher at school got to know who I was. The best part is that the Didi at Udaan got to know me at this point, and this felt like my biggest achievement because she was my first inspiration, and the feeling you get when your inspiration knows about your achievements is amazing.

As a topper, I would always focus on my studies. I never participated in any sports, events, or other things. When I entered class seven, my teacher told me I should participate in sports and other school events. Our PT sir told us about a

Kho-Kho competition and that he would choose girls for the competition. During the trials, he chose me over many others but was not very impressed by me, saying that some other girls were much more active in sports in general and so were better than me. When he started training us, though, he realised that I was genuinely a good player. He gave me the nickname of ajgar (python) and named me captain of my school kho-kho team. We won 1st prize in Kho-Kho. That moment as winning captain was unforgettable.

After completing class eight, I got admission to a new school. In this school, there were four sections: A, B, C and D. I got section D, where teachers treated the students like the weakest class in the whole school. At first, teachers thought that, like the other students, I was not good at studies. After the first internal exams, though, when I scored good marks in all subjects and topped in class, the teacher's way of thinking changed, and I became everyone's favourite. I became known in the whole school.

Then, my English teacher challenged us one day, declaring that in D division, no one would score above 80% in class 10. This motivated me to work hard and try to score a good percentage on my SSC Board. I got 86% for the SSC Board and topped my class. This year, I graduated with a BSc in IT. Now, my goal is to clear the UPSC exam and become an IAS officer to help everyone and make my family, friends, Udaan, and Mamta Didi proud.

Remember: The Harder you work, the luckier you get.

Regards,
Chanda

Dilip's Story

Dear Reader,

I have always been fascinated by the world of elements and compounds, and my passion for understanding chemical reactions drives me to learn more every day. That's why I am studying Chemistry in college.

I am from a small village in Uttar Pradesh. My mother and father are not very well educated. Still, they gave a lot of importance to education. They have always encouraged me to chase my dreams and have been my biggest supporters. My elder brother and sister helped me in my studies in the early days. They helped me a lot in my primary education. At this stage, I realised that I enjoy studying science subjects.

Chemistry, in particular, has a very different kind of theory with fun practicals. I am also fond of poetry, oratory, and stories.

This journey has not been without challenges. One was shifting from my village to Mumbai in 2017 due to some family and financial problems. Initially, it was difficult to adjust to the strict demands of school and the education system of Mumbai. Some time passed, and everything became balanced.

My dream is to contribute to scientific research, especially in the development of new substances or the discovery of sustainable chemical processes. Also, I want to help with the security of the country by doing research in advanced chemical labs in India, such as DRDO. At present, my focus is on various types of projects and the acquisition of skills, along with studies.

Till now, my family and friends have stayed with me on the path of life. With their support and love, the upcoming milestones will also pass smoothly.

The path of this life is special; there may be clouds of sadness, but they will go away.

Regards,
Dilip

SUMIT'S STORY

Dear Reader,

I was born in the vibrant city of Mumbai and grew up in a slum where every day was a fight for survival. The first few years of my life went by without much understanding of what lay ahead. When I reached sixth grade, I was faced with a harsh reality: bullying. My classmates constantly tormented me, making school a place of dread. I confided in my family, and my mother's advice was clear: 'Leave those friends behind. They'll only ruin your life'.

So, I did. I pulled away from everyone, retreating into isolation. I stopped playing outside and stopped talking to people. It was just me and my thoughts. But the bullying didn't stop. It haunted me, even when I was alone. Eventually, in eighth grade, I switched schools, hoping for a fresh start. Adjusting to the new environment was tough – new rules, new people, and the fear of facing the same rejection. But by ninth grade, I started opening up again, finding comfort with my tuition friends. That small circle became my escape, a place where I felt a sense of belonging.

Just as I was beginning to find my footing, life threw another curveball – the COVID-19 pandemic. Our family, like many others, was hit hard by financial struggles, and the world came to a standstill. But for me, the isolation felt strangely familiar. I had been through it before. Yet, the pressure to succeed mounted.

I studied hard, hoping to excel in my 10th-grade exams, but my results were not what I had hoped for, and our financial situation only worsened.

In desperation, I took up a job at a medical store.

After five months of work, I earned only 3,000 rupees. It felt like a small drop in an ocean of need, but it was something. I didn't let the disappointment break me. I went on to complete my 11th and 12th grades in the science stream, where I met a friend who would become like a brother to me.

We pursued a B Sc in Data Science together, sharing not only the challenges of academic life but also countless moments of joy. We laughed without a care in the world – on the streets, in class, and during our many adventures. These memories will stay with me forever.

It was during this time that one of my classmates told me about Udaan, an organisation that offers skills training. Udaan changed my life, not just by teaching me new skills but also by giving me the confidence I had lost over the years. Udaan provided me with a scholarship, which lifted a huge burden off my family's shoulders. Thanks to Udaan, I realised that setbacks don't define you; your resilience does.

Now, I'm working alongside my friend in his business, using everything I've learned to help it grow. I also tutor students at home to earn some pocket money, but what truly matters most is seeing my parents smile. They've been through so much, and every time I manage to make them laugh, even for a moment, it feels like a victory. Bringing them that joy is more rewarding than anything else.

As I look ahead, my aim is simple: to grow my friend's business or eventually become a businessman myself. But beyond success, what I truly seek is peace – peace of mind, peace in my heart, and the fulfilment that comes from knowing I've done right by the people I love.

Life has been unpredictable, but through it all, I've learned that it's not the hardships that define us, but how we choose to rise above them. My journey is just beginning, and with every step, I grow more determined to find not just success but peace.

Sincerely,
Sumit

Ashish's Story

Dear Readers,

I'm 18 years old, currently pursuing my B Com and I am in my second year. I consider myself a pretty average person – not too smart, not too dumb. But there are two things I truly love: writing and talking. I find it incredibly satisfying whenever I get the chance to express something, especially about myself. Bringing my thoughts into words takes a special kind of effort, and I enjoy it a lot. Additionally, I have a deep passion for sketching anime characters, something I've been doing since the 5th standard and continue to enjoy today. Today, I'm taking a step forward by penning down a small story about parts of my life.

My family is a mix of different personalities, each with his or her own path. My father is the one who handles all the loans and is already planning to travel after retirement. My mother, the one who takes care of the house, just wants everyone to be happy so she can finally relax. My eldest brother is so focused on shining in life that he sometimes forgets to take care of himself. Recently, a new member joined our family – my sister-in-law. Though I don't know much about her yet, she's quite different from the typical modern-day girls and is loved by everyone at home. Then there's my middle brother, Deepak, who wants to break away from our family's traditions and do something big. And then there's me, someone who doesn't know exactly what to do but is content with what I have.

My parents originally lived in a village, but my father, thinking out of the box for the first time, moved us to Mumbai. At first, we lived near the mountains, though I don't remember much of that time. My brothers often remind me of those days. After I was born, they bought a flat, and we've been living here ever since.

Now, I want to do something out of the box like my father did and take them to a better place, to show them that I'm capable of achieving big things. I want to show my mother the world, to take her out of the house, as she rarely steps out. I haven't figured out exactly what I want to become yet, but I know I want to do something significant. In childhood, I didn't have any particular dreams, but when PUBG became popular, I was fascinated by it and wanted to be a game developer and create new games. Later, I thought about becoming an eSports player. For years, I've considered becoming an animator. Sometimes, I feel like learning to code because I enjoy working on my laptop.

My dream is to visit Japan and South Korea once in my lifetime – South Korea for a short trip, but I'd like to spend more time in Japan. I'll need to earn money to achieve that and figuring out how to do that is the next step. And I will make it happen, no matter what. My hopes are simple: I want my parents to see me as successful and happy. I want to take them on trips because family issues have always kept us confined at home. But I hope, and I believe, that things will get better soon.

When it comes to my journey, I'd say I haven't faced many problems that I have had to overcome on my own. My family has never let big problems arise in my life. Everything was fine until 10th grade, but in 11th grade, I met some friends I wish I hadn't met. Because of them, I developed a habit of going out a lot.

While there's nothing wrong with exploring, lying to my parents about it wasn't right. I had an attitude problem back then, even with my brothers. I visited places like Mumbra Devi, Marine Drive, and Ambernath. It seems like the gods of Ambernath wanted me to stop because, after that, my parents found out.

Because of my behaviour, the trust I had built with my family over the years was shattered in an instant. They never expected that their little 'Babu' would do something like that. From that day, I wasn't 'Babu' anymore, and that's something I still regret. But even here, I didn't overcome the situation on my own. God sent me a friend, who made those friends drift away from me, and I'm lucky that happened. By luck, she is still with me. That's why I say I've never really overcome anything on my own – someone always comes along to save me. Since then, I haven't gone out much, but when I want to, I do it with permission and without lies.

If there's one thing I could use help with, it's figuring out what I can do. I want someone to tell me my options and where I fit in. My middle brother could guide me, but he's busy, so I don't ask him. But I really want to get serious about my future and career. I don't want to sacrifice my present, but I need to create a rough blueprint of my future so I can decide what I want to do. I prefer learning things practically, like through workshops, but I don't get such opportunities. I try to find them, but they're hard to come by. I want to discover something that gives me an idea of what I can do. I'm still that confused kid. I just want a simple and sweet life with my parents and loved ones. But making that simple and sweet life doesn't seem so easy.

Thanks for taking the time to read this part of my life.

Ashish

SUSHMA'S STORY

Dear Reader,

There are five siblings in my family. My parents worked hard to take care of us and have given their best to help us achieve our goals.

In my childhood, I wasn't very outgoing. I was a quiet, introverted girl who didn't do well in my studies. This fear led to me becoming very shy and timid. Then, I joined Udaan in 2007 and felt comfortable there. This was a turning point, and I couldn't be more grateful for the transformation it brought in me as a person and in my life. The teachers were great, and they explained things in a very simple way, which made learning easier for me. When I passed 10th standard, my parents were the happiest, and my Udaan Didi was also very happy. Some people thought I wouldn't be able to pass, but my parents and Udaan believed in me, and I did it. This was the happiest moment of my life.

Then, I continued my studies while doing an assistant teacher internship at Udaan. I joined Udaan for an internship in 2013. During this time, I learned a lot of things – one thing I like about myself is that I pick up new things quickly. I feel deeply grateful to my Udaan Didi for being such a guiding force and mentor in my life. She has been like a guru to me, guiding me through the ECCEd Diploma course and providing valuable support throughout the journey. My transformation from a shy, under-confident person to an extremely confident person who is capable of holding her own and guiding others is largely due to the role Udaan played in my life. I love guiding kids by giving them the things I didn't get in my childhood – an innovative, creative, and safe environment and easy ways of learning.

My family, friends, and Udaan have contributed the most to my journey, and I will always be grateful to them. Their support and belief in me have been invaluable, guiding me through every step and helping me become the person I am today. All of them have played a crucial role in shaping my path, and I carry their influence with me in all that I do.

Thank you,
Sushma

DIPANSHU'S STORY

Dear Reader,

I am a 21-year-old with roots in Mumbai but who was born in the humble soil of Nanded, Maharashtra. My life began in a village where even basic necessities like electricity and water were out of reach. My parents, however, had a dream to soar above the trying circumstances around us – a dream to provide me and my two younger sisters with a future far brighter than the life they had known. Sixteen years ago, they took a leap of faith and moved to Mumbai, hoping to rewrite our destiny.

Koshish karne walon ki kabhi haar nahi hoti,
Andhiyon se ladne wale, chhaya mein kabhi par nahi phailate.

But Mumbai was not the escape we had imagined. Though we had a house here, my uncle and aunt refused to let us in, turning our refuge into a battleground. They were ruthless, often showing up at our doorstep armed with threats and weapons. I was merely seven or eight years old, forced to witness these horrors. My nights were sleepless, and my parents were vigilant in protecting us. For five to six long years, our life was a series of battles, each night more terrifying than the last.

Yet, even amidst this turmoil, my parents never let go of one thing – our education. They held on to the belief that

'Education is the key to breaking the chains of poverty'. Their resilience and determination were the pillars that held me up. Inspired by accounts of the lives of Dr B R Ambedkar and Dr A P J Abdul Kalam, I found solace, and purpose in my studies. I excelled in school, ranking first consistently from 1st to 10th grade. Education became my sanctuary, allowing me to dream without fear.

Sapno se apne khud ko judne do,
Udaan toh wohi bharte hai, jo zameen se uddne do.

In the 8th grade, just as I was preparing for a crucial scholarship exam, life threw yet another curveball. I was struck by seizures, collapsing without warning and losing consciousness for minutes that felt like hours. My family was financially crippled, unable to afford the necessary treatment. But, as fate would have it, my school principal intervened, ensuring I received the medical care I desperately needed. This illness changed me. I withdrew from my friends, gave up cricket, and confined myself to a life within the walls of my home.

Despite these limitations, a flicker of hope emerged when I was selected to participate in the Republic Day parade with the Scouts. Held at Dadar Shivaji Park in the presence of the Mayor of Mumbai, it was a moment of immense pride. Living in a camp away from home for 15-20 days was a challenge. I feared that a seizure could strike me at any moment, but I persevered. Marching in that parade was more than just a source of pride; it was a victory over my fears and circumstances.

Manzil unhi ko milti hai jinke sapno mein jaan hoti hai,
Pankh se kuch nahi hota, hauslon se udaan hoti hai.

Time went on, and the struggles continued. I passed my 10th grade with 2nd rank and received scholarships that helped ease our financial burdens. My dream was to become a surgeon. I attempted the NEET exam twice, aiming for a seat in a government medical college, but fate had other plans. Accepting my reality, I turned to Biotechnology. Here, too, financial constraints loomed large, but a benevolent soul, Dr Bhandarkar, funded my education. It is because of his kindness that I was able to complete my degree.

Today, I find myself at a crossroads. I've taken a gap year to truly understand my calling. My aspiration is to become a civil servant, to serve my country, and to extend a helping hand to those in need – just as many have extended a helping hand to me. My father, now past 52, has carried the weight of our family for too long. It is my turn to shoulder that burden. I currently take up tutoring and internships to support my family while my sisters continue their education. My journey has shaped me into who I am, and it is far from over.

Chalne se hi banta hai safar, rukne se nahi,
Raaste wohi milenge, jo kabhi khoya nahi.

'Success is not final, and failure is not fatal: It is the courage to continue that counts.' If my story can light a spark in even one heart, if it can inspire someone to rise above their circumstances and chase their dreams, then every hardship I have endured will have been worth it.

With hope and determination,

Dipanshu

MUKESH'S STORY

Dear Reader,

This is a letter for those like me from someone who struggled for 10 years of academics and is now trying to grow and achieve success.

I was a very shy and introverted guy, never believing I would come this far. My early life was typical of a middle-class, ambitious child who didn't know what to do. I got 63% in class 10 – very average. I never knew how to understand concepts or 'how to study'. My parents were so upset when they had to pay extra to get me admission into class 11th.

After this admission, in my sorrow, I started watching a lot of YouTube, and it helped me a lot. Channels like Sandeep Maheshwari, Vivek Bindra, Aman Dhattarwal, The Ranveer Show, Figuring Out, Gaur Gopal Das, and others gave me insights into life, personality, people, love, and studies. I realised that, 'If you want to open up in social events, you need to have command over something – whether a subject, topic, or skill'. This created a hunger for learning in me.

Eventually, I found myself at Udaan India Foundation, an NGO that gave me hope, independence, learning, and care. After 12th, I joined their basic computer course. The activities – explaining topics, presenting, and group communication – all shaped my confidence, communication, presentation skills, and personality.

With each course and internship, I continued to learn. I was fortunate to meet a mentor, a nature lover, who supported me emotionally and personally when I was off track, frustrated, and depressed. One message of his that stuck with me was that, *Jo mera hai, wo mujhe milke rahega, aur jo mera nahi hai, uske piche mai kitna bhi chalu, wo nahi milega* (What is meant for me will come to me, and what is not mine, no matter how much I chase it, I won't get it).

That message brought me back on track. I continued to self-learn graphic design and video editing, watch podcasts on YouTube, and grow as a person. After my graduation, I got a part-time job opportunity with Udaan, followed by a full-time job from a connection I made at Udaan.

In the end, I realised that if I had let every problem stop me, I would still be the same person I was in class 10 – dumb and boring. I'm grateful for every obstacle, every person, every YouTube channel, and all the luck and energy I have had for shaping me. I've learned to understand the mistakes of others and of my own and avoid repeating them, and I've embraced the power of manifestation, good karma, patience, purity in myself, and true care. Now, I'm 21 and figuring out, helping, learning, and going with good thoughts.

Thank You.
Regards,
Mukesh

GANGA'S STORY

Dear Readers,

I'm a very energetic and excitement-filled girl who loves dancing and travelling. Yes, there are a few hurdles, but I feel very good when my father helps me sometimes, and I am able to make decisions on my own. I also like to make friends, but my father thinks that friends are selfish and ultimately look after their own interests. But it is not like that; there are also some good friends.

If I have to say something at my home, I will say that I want to do everything that I really like, so that in the future I don't regret losing opportunities that I should have taken.

Talking about my own family, I currently live with my adoptive mom and dad. Earlier I lived in Pune, where my birth mother, father, and my four brothers lived. When I was little, my father gave me to his sister, i.e., my aunt, and from then on, she became my guardian. Since then, I have been living with her in Mumbai.

Papa goes to work in the morning and comes home in the evening. Mummy, on the other hand, is all day like a strict teacher. But they are great the way they are. My family was very good earlier. But some things happen unexpectedly and without reason that are not under our control.

When Papa fell ill and was admitted to the hospital, things got worse. It seems as if nothing has gone well after that.

Papa's health deteriorated and at one point, his memory also started getting affected. After many treatments, Papa became healthy, but there was not as much life and strength inside him anymore. Because of this, my parents' behaviour towards me changed a lot. Mummy struggled to talk properly, and Papa would get upset over small things. I don't know what I had done wrong.

Till date, small and big problems keep coming in life, but my Mummy and Papa never stopped us from moving ahead. But problems… it seems like they never end. When one problem ends, another comes at the door. Mummy and Papa get stressed out and are unable to think positively. Because of these things, there have been a lot of fights in the house, but we have managed everything and did not let anything go wrong.

We all are trying to give our best from our side so that we can become the same as we were before. Papa still goes to do his work, but due to age, he is not able to work like he used to. Mummy does as much as she can at home, but she has become a typical old woman. She was not like this earlier. Maybe she became like this because of society. Earlier, when Mummy was young, she used to wear jeans, my mummy was modern, but not anymore. Mummy knows a lot of things, like operating a telephone booth, running a kindergarten, and many other jobs. But while managing the house, perhaps she forgot all about them.

Along with my studies, I do small part-time jobs so that I can meet my expenses and not trouble them. I am not interested in my studies; I like to acquire practical knowledge.

If I were to describe my story in brief, I would say it's been a roller coaster.

Where I got a chance to take part in college projects like BBBS (Big Brother Big Sister) and got the experience of meeting such a nice ma'am, all this was unexpected and so amazing that I could not even have imagined. If I had not sat in that event that day, maybe I would never have got this chance. As a Big Sister, I told the little kids and taught them what is good touch, bad touch and how to treat each other. Some children wanted to become good from the beginning, but for those who did not know anything about all these things, our BBBS took the first step towards improvement.

Then, as an NSS volunteer, I got a chance to stay in a college camp for 7 days. This is one of the best moments of my life. Because the view there was unforgettable. Which I will never forget. And that waterfall was very beautiful. I found things by myself in that jungle, lit a fire and cooked food, I got such experiences and learnt many things which I will never forget. We all stayed in a Vridhashram (old age home) there, and seeing them, my perspective changed completely. I worry about them, and I think that I will never become like those children who leave their parents there and go away. I will show them by becoming their super daughter.

It is dream time!

I want to do modelling, but I don't know where to start. First of all, I want to buy a new phone with my own money. Then, along with studies, I want to pursue modelling so that I can tell my parents that I can also do something. And finally, I want to represent India once in my life.

And I also want to travel a lot out of the country, but I do not want to take permission from anyone. I don't want to have to depend on others to do the things I want. I want to do everything I want to do.

And I never have to think about money.

I have so many dreams, and I just hope I get a chance to fulfil some of them.

Regards,
Ganga

AASIYA'S STORY

Dear Reader,

I am a 23-year-old aspiring Chartered Accountant from Mumbai – a city where dreams are as plentiful as the traffic jams. My story began in a humble family, where I faced financial hardships but had abundant love and support. Despite our economic struggles, my parents always believed in my potential. Further, the support of Didi and Bhaiya from Udaan truly helped me soar.

When I was growing up, my family's financial crises nearly halted my education. During 12th grade, I met a Didi from Udaan, who first asked, 'What do you want to become?' That was a question I had never asked myself. She didn't just ask for the sake of asking; she believed in me. She taught me that my personality, passion, and perseverance were more important than just a degree. Her words lit a fire in me. She believed in me when I didn't believe in myself.

Udaan became a beacon of hope, offering financial aid and a network of mentors who encouraged me to dream bigger. Udaan gave me a community. Ratna Didi, a mentor and friend through Udaan, played a crucial role in my journey. Her unwavering belief in me has pushed me through the hardest times. She always says, 'Your dreams are valid, no matter where you come from'. Her belief in me helped me get through this journey.

Passing each level of the CA course has been a victory, not just academically but also emotionally. There were challenges, of course. I was an introvert, shy and unsure of myself, but my journey through the Udaan and the CA course changed me. The intense workload, the endless deadlines, and the need to deal with various kinds of people and colleagues forced me to break out of my shell. Over time, I grew from an introvert to an ambivert, finding a balance between solitude and social engagement.

I am proud of this transformation because it taught me that growth often comes from discomfort. I also battled some health issues early on, which could have derailed my studies, but instead, they made me stronger and more determined. I have faced challenges, especially when I failed an attempt. It was disheartening, but I realised that failure is a steppingstone to success. I picked myself up, analysed where I went wrong, and worked harder the next time. It taught me perseverance, time management, and the importance of believing in myself.

My fascination with numbers led me to pursue a career in a CA course. However, my ambitions extend beyond becoming a CA. I envision myself as a top executive, making strategic decisions to drive growth and create value.

Additionally, I am committed to giving back to the community that supported me, volunteering my time and resources to help children, much like Udaan helped me. Travelling to explore the world is also a dream I aspire towards. My friends have been a vital and beautiful support system, standing by me through every failure and success. They remind me that while achieving goals is important, the journey itself shapes who we are. Though my journey is still unfolding, I remain eager to master leadership, public speaking, and financial strategy. I hope to connect with mentors and peers who can guide and inspire me further.

Thank you for taking the time to read my story. My journey is still unfolding, and I can't wait to see where it leads.

Gratefully and affectionately,

Aasiya

Aditi's Story

Dear Reader,

I am from a middle-class family. My father is a carpenter, and my mother is a housewife. I am 16 years old. There are eight people in my family. I have five sisters and a younger brother. Only my father can manage such a large family.

I want to become a data analyst. My dream is to go to Kedarnath with my whole family and visit all of Mahadev's temples. I dream of seeing my father sitting in his office, drinking tea, saying, 'my daughter did it'. I have big dreams and want to fulfil them to make my father happy.

I cannot explain my life in one go, as there are many different stories in my life, some of which have brought me happiness, others bringing me sorrow. Some stories have also built my confidence and pride. Udaan has been a key part of these stories.

I studied in a government school from first to tenth grade. When the lockdown came, it threatened to disrupt our studies, but Udaan supported us a lot by giving us phones so that we could attend online classes and our studies would continue. I joined Udaan in eighth grade and was initially very scared, but the Didis at Udaan supported me a lot and told me that I could do everything.

I passed tenth grade with 82% marks. Today, I am in one of the top colleges here, studying Commerce.

I want to make everyone understand that girls are no less than boys – they can achieve whatever they decide to accomplish. Udaan and my family are supporting me in fulfilling my dream. In this 16-year journey of mine, I have learned that the moment you start thinking clearly about your dream, you will start to gain success. However, you have to work hard. In life, we will have companions and support, but we must ultimately fight for our dreams ourselves. Just as there is morning after night, there is a proud feeling that we did it.

Yours lovingly,
Aditi

GAURAV'S STORY

Dear Reader,

I see myself as a traveller who doesn't know which paths are ahead and which paths to choose but goes forward with courage, driven by the knowledge that the Lord is with him.

Let me give more info about me. I am one of my parents' five children and am treated as the special child because I am the elder brother of my four sisters. I am from a middle-class family, but I am blessed that I don't have to cry about anything and that the Lord never leaves our side.

As I said, I would describe myself as a traveller, but I would also describe my life as a seesaw. It might sound funny – saying first that I am blessed and now saying that my life is a seesaw, i.e. (full of ups and downs). What I would say to that is that whether it is a poor person or a rich person, both will have some problems in their life. i.e., no one's life is stable on earth.

So, why did I call my life a seesaw?

I would start from the beginning: when I was in kindergarten, I was a very poor student. I had a friend named Rituraj who, to be honest, was more studious than me. At that time, I was upset that I was not so good, but when I went to the 1st standard, I joined a home tuition programme in my area. The tutor was strict, so I eventually grew in all aspects of my studies. It was the first achievement of my life. Then, a girl named Rashi was admitted, and I got competition in my studies. We competed over who was best in studies, encouraging me to work harder. I became the topper in my school.

But then, one day in 7th standard, the home tuition got closed and I got lost in a superficial, materialistic world, which was my downfall. It feels like I was in the sky and came down to the depths of the ocean after leaving that home tuition. This is the stage at which I went on the wrong path, which became worse because people treated me like hell.

From this time till 10th standard, I was an average student, but then in the 11th standard, I joined a class where I found a sir and mentor who guided and supported me, and I again started growing myself. Though I was good in my studies, I lacked other skills. Because of that, I lost many opportunities. Then, I joined the Udaan India Foundation, which led to growth in my personality and digital skills. Now, I am very capable of leading in any situation.

This was just about my educational journey. Apart from this, I have had many ups and downs in different circumstances. In the end, the message I want to convey is that ups and downs are part of life. We might feel grateful for some things, and other things might seem unwanted, but we should have courage. If the Lord closes a door, he opens a hundred windows, and we will see them if we have courage and patience.

Thank You.

Gaurav

GOPAL'S STORY

Dear Readers,

I live with my joint family in Mumbai. I'm studying for a B Sc in IT and am currently in my final year. Right now, I'm preparing for my final exams, and at the same time, I'm taking some online courses to improve my skills.

I want to become a software engineer. This is my biggest dream, and I hope to get a good job to help me achieve everything I've planned. I also have a bucket list of things I want to do. I want to give my family a stable and happy life and help my parents enjoy their retirement without any stress.

Besides my studies, I love to enjoy life. I like going on trips with my family and friends, exploring new places, and learning about them. I also enjoy playing online games, which is a fun way for me to relax and recharge.

So far, my life has been pretty good. I've faced some challenges with my studies, especially during COVID and the lockdown, but I got through them and stayed focused on my goals. I'm proud to say that I'm better than before, in my studies and my outlook on life. Over time, I've grown more mature and now understand things better.

Apart from studies, I'm also learning about things like investing in the right places and creating two or more income sources in my life. I'm slowly gaining knowledge about these areas so I can be financially secure in the future.

This is my story, and my journey is still going on. With the support of my family and friends, and my dreams always driving me, I believe I'll reach my goals.

Regards,
Gopal

Khushboo's Story

Dear Reader,

When I was small, I was very mischievous, and I used to have a lot of fun like everyone else. But I always used to have a little too much fun when I went with my friends to the park. One day, I fell while doing some tricks and got a head injury. The injury was very deep, and a lot of blood was flowing.

I lost consciousness, and when everyone got to know, they came to my house. Right after that, mummy tried to relieve the fever, but after some time, I started vomiting. My parents then felt that I wouldn't get healed so easily, so they took me to a doctor. Then, the doctor checked and gave me medicine, telling me I needed to take it. Anyway, I didn't like the medicine, so when I went back home to rest, I told my mummy I didn't want to take it. Mummy asked me what happened, and I smiled and said I would be alright without medicine, as God was with us. I also said that we should be positive, as what happens depends on what we believe will happen.

I didn't know what was going to happen. I thought I would definitely be fine, even without medicine. When my mummy brought me medicine, I would tell her I didn't need it, and that became my mindset. After some days, a miracle happened – I became completely fine. The doctor was shocked that anyone could get well so quickly. I understood that my positive mindset was the biggest reason I overcame the illness without medication. Whether you trust others or not, trusting yourself is necessary.

Along with trust in yourself, trust in others is also crucial. It drives everything when you think about it. Doctors cure patients due to the patient's trust in them; our parents' trust in each other keeps our families together and teaches us many things. This is seen in other species, too – birds like the albatross, a large bird that flies very high in the sky, practice monogamy, and trust their partners for life. The importance of trust has been a key lesson for me.

Regards,
Khushboo

Pooja's Story

Dear Readers,

As I sit down to pen this letter for *Apna Time Aayega*, I think of my life as an opera – a series of musical acts filled with both exciting highs and quiet moments. I am currently navigating my second year of a BCA programme, fervently aspiring to become a software developer.

Imagine an opera with its varied acts and arias. This metaphor resonates deeply with my life so far. Each phase has been a unique song, sometimes joyful, other times reflective and calm. These songs are not just experiences but deeply felt emotions, portraying the complexities and richness of my journey.

The story began with a burst of enthusiasm, filled with dreams as vast as the sky. The early melodies were characterized by a carefree, energetic tune—symbolizing the excitement of new beginnings and the thrill of academic adventures. These were the days when every line of code I learned felt like a step toward the future I had always envisioned.

As the opera progressed, there were moments when the music softened, turning into a more introspective symphony. These silent storms, though less visible to the outside world, were moments of self-doubt, struggle, and growth.

Yet, it is in these silent phases that I discovered resilience and strength. They taught me the invaluable lesson that even in stillness, progress is made. In the middle of these changing melodies, there has always been one constant source of harmony—my family. To my family, I extend my deepest gratitude. Your unwavering support and belief in my dreams have been the bedrock of my journey. Each note of encouragement, every gesture of love, has been a vital part of this opera. I also owe a special thank you to Udaan, my 'Second Home', that has been instrumental in providing me with opportunities to grow and learn beyond the conventional classroom. Udaan's role in my life has been like the chorus of the opera – supporting and enhancing the main melody with its contributions.

Furthermore, I want to acknowledge everyone who has supported me, both directly and indirectly. To my friends, mentors, and even the kind strangers whose small acts of kindness have left lasting impressions – your support has been like the subtle, uplifting harmonies that complete a symphony.

Looking ahead, my aspirations are grand. I dream of making a mark as a software developer, but my goals extend beyond career achievements. I strive to be a good human being, someone who contributes positively to the world around me.

This will be the final act of my opera, where the culmination of all experiences and aspirations creates a beautiful and meaningful melody. As I continue to compose the symphony of my life, I hope that my story will inspire others to embrace their own journeys—whether their melodies are loud or soft, joyful or reflective. Remember, every phase is a part of your opera, and each note, no matter how small, adds to the magnificence of your life's composition.

Thank you for being a part of my journey. Here's to composing many more beautiful melodies together.

With gratitude and hope,
Pooja

KHUSHI'S STORY

Dear Reader,

I live in Mumbai with my sister. I'm pursuing the last year of my degree as a Medical Lab Technician. I want to do the best I can in my field, and while, at times, I find it a struggle to keep up with my studies, especially theory, I remind myself that I need to focus.

That focus comes from being aware of where I am coming from and my expectations. As a child, I got to know that my father had a dream of becoming a doctor, and had fulfilled it, but then he had to let go of that dream. I saw how much he struggled and sacrificed to bring us up and provide a good life and education for us, and while I never got to know what circumstances had made him give up on his dream, I decided that my father's dream would now be mine. I am working to fulfil it, no matter how hard it may seem at times.

While there have been challenges in my journey, with my family's support, I have managed to make progress towards fulfilling my dream. As I've grown older, I've realised that sometimes the biggest challenges are the ones we ourselves put in our way. In my case, that has sometimes been my unwillingness to face reality when things are not going well. I have been working on fixing that and becoming more mature and stronger so that no matter what obstacles or setbacks I face, I can deal with them with kindness and humility.

I am not much of a talker, so it's hard for me to express everything I feel, but I do put down my thoughts in my diary, as writing things down makes it feel like I'm letting go of burdens and sharing them.

My story is a simple one, and my dream is a simple one. I want to fulfil my father's dream and create a better life for my family. I have a long way to go, but I am on my way!

Thank you!
Khushi

Krishna's Story

Dear Reader,

I am 19 years old. I am from Karnataka but was born in Mumbai. There are seven members in my family. I live with my Mumma, Papa, three brothers, and one sister.

My elder brother is working as a delivery boy in an office. He wanted to become a tattoo artist, but due to some financial issues, he couldn't complete his tattoo artist course. My second oldest brother works as an office boy for a company. My father is a carpenter, and my mother is a housewife. My third brother is younger than me, in the 8th standard, and loves playing cricket. Finally, my sister is a first-year student, studying for BA (Bachelor of Arts). She wants to become a teacher.

I am now about to complete my graduation in Bachelor of Science in Information Technology. I want to become a software engineer. I hope to get a good job after my graduation with a good package, so that my family can depend on me. My dream is to make my parents proud of me so that they see me as someone who can fulfil their dreams. I want to work hard so that my parents can rest and enjoy life, without the pressures that they are facing right now.

I am a hodophile. I would love to travel around the whole world. Another hobby of mine is origami, especially making flowers with paper.

My journey has been very challenging. Since my childhood, though, I have had friends who have stood by me at all times, which has helped me deal with challenges. When I was in grade four, I had an accident that damaged my eyes. I was living in the Hiranandani layout at the time, and my friends, my elder brother, and I found a packet of gunpowder near DMart. We did not know what it was, so we started burning a small amount of it, which had no effect on us. Soon, though, we had burned the whole packet, which was way too much. We got injured; I almost lost my eyes, and my elder brother got scars on his face and shoulder. One of our friends also got brutally injured, with scars on his back, and was about to lose his life. Crying, I ran to my parents, who were shocked and started crying too. They called an ambulance, and we went to the hospital. We were in hospital for many days, and during this time, my mama would make us feel better, play with us every morning, and tease us.

Besides these memories, I have good memories of my first to 6th standard, as I was lucky to have good friends who I would enjoy a lot with. In the 7th standard, for some reason, I had to change schools because my older brother studied in another school, and he had his Boards. This was hard for me because I lost some of my friends due to this change. However, I adjusted soon to the new school and made friends who are still with me.

Through all of this, if there was a place I could call home, it was Udaan. It isn't a school but an organisation that works with students to make them independent and financially capable of doing something big. I can say proudly that I am still a part of Udaan India Foundation. It's a place where I have met many friends who have become like family. Over time, they have changed, but their behaviour towards me never changed, and they have helped me in tough times.

There is one friend in particular who played a very important role in my life, and I am blessed to have that one friend. She helped me emotionally and made me mentally strong and responsible. I met her through Udaan in the 8th standard. When I passed 12th standard, I got demotivated as I got low marks. Due to that, my parents scolded me, and I felt like I was about to lose everything. She was there, though, to make me believe that it wasn't so dire.

My college admission wasn't very good, but it wasn't the worst either. I started working on my studies and got 91% in the first year and 92% in the second year. Now, I have my Boards next month. Although I am worried, I know I can do well this time too. As a person, I have some positive aspects, such as how I can make anyone laugh and my interest in hobbies like origami. I want to learn more things, though, like discipline, consistency, and skills like programming, which can help me in the future.

Thank you.

Krishna

Priyanka's Story

Dear Reader,

It feels good to listen to this story, but it was much more difficult to experience it.

This is not just a story but someone's complete life, a journey from childhood to youth. It is about finding hope in hopelessness. Dying is very easy, but living is difficult, that too in such a city where everyone judges you. But, as they say, God gives everyone a chance. Udaan and the Didi at Udaan gave me that chance.

When I was in the 4th standard in a municipal school with my brothers, I remember there being no money for food at home, no money for books, and there was a fight between mom and dad. In the meantime, my dreams were stuck. I used to wonder why we were like this and why all this was happening to us.

Mummy was teaching me as well as she could. There wasn't any support from my papa, as he said that in his house, girls shouldn't be taught too much.

But my mother took steps to move forward and fought with everyone. At this time, she got to know about Udaan, and she got us admission. We didn't know English, so we started learning it. It felt great, and mummy was also happy that her kids were learning well.

A few years passed like this. Then, municipal schooling ended in the 7th standard, and we were given admission to a new school in the 8th standard. In our school, they treated us badly because we came from a municipal school, and they thought we didn't know anything. It is said that school is a place where there is no discrimination and no differences matter, but we felt it in the beginning. Eighth standard went by like this and my result wasn't very good. My turning point started in the 9th standard. They say that challenges are necessary for someone to fight with true resolve and stubbornness, and that's what my experience was.

One day, the computer period was going on, and the teacher called everyone to give a small speech on computers. I also raised my hand, but the teacher gave everyone else a chance to speak. I objected, but she shook her head, saying, 'What will you say? Anyways, I know how much English you municipal school kids know'.

I could not sleep the whole night, so hurt was I by this episode. This one line made me mature instantly and made me determined to prove her and others wrong who judged me and others like me just because of our background. Even today, while writing my hands are trembling and there are tears in my eyes. Years later, I did achieve what I had in mind. I got first rank in Maharashtra University of Health Sciences in Bachelor of Optometry, among a million students and the whole paper was in English!

In the ninth and 10th standards, I studied hard, and my teachers never believed at first how I was managing to get such good results. However, in the tenth, I encountered a big issue. Just a couple of days before my exams, both my brothers met with an accident. One could not walk; the other's leg was broken. I used to do all the work at home, then I had to take care of them, and I did not feel like giving the exams at all, but mummy convinced me to keep studying and appear for the exams.

When the results came, I was sure that I will pass, but I did not expect at all that I would get the second rank in the whole school. I began to dream of becoming a doctor, but when I discussed it with my mother, I wondered whether we would have enough money to fund that education. So, I took a Commerce form in college, but my mother insisted I not give up on my dreams, so I also took a Science form.

One day, at Udaan, Mamta Didi came and asked everyone what they wanted to study. So, I raised my hand for Commerce. Didi called me aside and asked why I wasn't taking Science as I had wanted to be a doctor. I caught hold of Mamta Didi and started crying and told her everything. She told me to take Science and not give up.

I took admission in college and I studied with full dedication. Didi helped with the fees for the classes. I used to go to college at 8 in the morning and return home at 11 pm after classes in the evening. I used to study for more than 15 hours, because I was not just studying Science, but dealing with the challenge of studying everything in English.

I wanted to take the NEET exam to be a doctor, but again, we were worried about the financial burden. At Udaan, some of our guides told me I could pursue a paramedical course, as it would cost less, and I could still serve at a hospital. I visited a few colleges and got admission to a medical college. I worked very hard, but new challenges came my way.

COVID marked the biggest change in my life. I have not told this to anyone till now. In 2020, my father and brother started saying we sisters should get married, and that there was no need to study. I took a small house in a chawl by paying Rs 5000 as rent and then I put all my life into completing my studies. I studied so much that I got 1st rank in the entire Maharashtra University of Health Sciences.

Now I am an eye-care professional, working as a senior Optometrist. I still have dreams to fulfil. I would like to buy my own home and do something for my country, but I feel good about never having given up and having the support of mentors at Udaan to support and guide me.

Regards
Priyanka

LAXMI'S STORY

Dear Reader,

I am at present a Lead teacher in MPS Varsha Nagar School.

From childhood, I was fascinated by teaching, and as I grew older, my curiosity led me to become a pre-primary teacher. I have faced many ups and downs during my journey, and Udaan India has helped me at every stage.

As a child, I was not very bright in my studies; I failed in 10th standard, and my struggles made me feel worthless. Thus, after class ten, I thought of giving up on my studies and going to the village to learn stitching. My family members encouraged me to do this, for they too had lost hope in my studies, but deep inside, I felt like I was not ready to accept defeat so easily.

Feeling lost, I went to my Didi at Udaan, who has supported me a lot, to speak about my results and her tight hug calmed me down.None of my family and friends had shown so much warmth at that time, and I had started to feel quite depressed. Her 'jaadu ki jhappi' as she calls it, warmed me, and she held my hand and told me she had faith in me to achieve success if I persevered. This changed my life.

I took admission in class eleven to give myself a second chance, and she guided me on the ATKT exam, which pre-graduation and graduation students can take if they fail. I passed grade 10 and grade 11 and shed tears of joy. I had not cried when I had failed, but now that I had made it through, all the emotions of the last year came flowing out of my brother, my mummy, and me. This experience gave me belief, and after this, I started believing and giving my best in everything.

I completed my MA in education in English from Mumbai University's ECCed programme from SM Shetty College. Now, I don't feel bad about myself; rather, I feel proud and believe that I am, in fact, a bright child. I can say all this proudly because of my Udaan. Udaan supported me and stood by me during this period and taught me never to give up, to have faith in myself, and to give my best until I succeed. It taught me that if I do this, I can achieve anything. Udaan birthed the positive spark in me and taught me that I can make a difference, so I am eternally grateful to them. Whatever I am today is thanks to them; without their financial support and guidance, I might not have been a teacher today and my dream would have remained unfulfilled. Thank you, Udaan India Foundation, for making my story a successful one.

Regards,
Laxmi

Mahak's Story

Dear Reader,

I was born in Mumbai, a city where everyone has their own story. Since my childhood, I have been surrounded by my loving family, of which I am the eldest child.

When I was growing up, my parents were my rock, providing a foundation of stability and encouragement that shaped me into the person I am today. Meanwhile, my siblings have been my best friends. I was one of the brilliant students in my school-good at studies, well-mannered, and disciplined. On the other hand, I was introverted.

I completed my tenth and 12th standards with good marks. After completing my 12th standard, I went to Indore and spent my summer vacation there, enjoying a lot.

After I came back from Indore, my father told me about the Udaan India Foundation and told me to join the computer skills batch. This was a turning point in my life. The day I visited Udaan, I met Shailesh Bhaiya. At first, I thought he was strict, but when we started discussing about Udaan and choosing courses after 12th standard, I got to know how helpful he is.

I was unaware that the place I was stepping into would completely change me. After I joined the computer batch, I met Anurag bhaiya and I thought that getting a different facilitator who didn't know me wouldn't be good. However, I found him to be very supportive. He had understood that I was an introvert and encouraged me to get involved in group discussions.

Next, I got the wonderful opportunity to learn from Sushree Didi and Priyanka Didi. Their simple and engaging explanations helped us understand things more easily. After doing more courses, I met Rati Didi, whose support and valuable advice made me a person I had never thought I would be. Didi started encouraging me to participate in every activity. Whenever I would say, 'Didi, will I be able to do this?' Didi always said, 'Why not? Just give it a try'. This really took my confidence to another level. Her support made me go an extra mile in whatever I did. I feel immensely grateful for her support and guidance.

Also, I learned a lot from Priya Ma'am, a facilitator known for her calm mind and helping nature. Hasti Didi also supported me in pursuing what I wanted to. I gained more confidence, improved my communication skills, and had wonderful opportunities to have corporate visits, among other benefits. Finally, a day came when my efforts and my facilitators' efforts paid off. I was awarded the titles of 'Torch bearer of Udaan' and 'Ace communicator', which was the biggest achievement of my life till then.

I'm still working on myself and also working to achieve my dreams and goals, and I will always be grateful to all the amazing facilitators at Udaan who have changed my life.

Regards,
Mahak

Nikesh's Story

Dear Reader,

I never imagined such a simple question – What Next? – would change my life and lead me in a completely new direction!

I began my studies in my hometown, Jaunpur, Uttar Pradesh. It's a beautiful place, with everything one imagines when thinking of a village: a small river, a giant forest on one side, and a mango orchard nearby. I got the opportunity to relocate to Mumbai, becoming the first in my extended family to move to the city for studies. However, due to a lack of proper certification, I struggled to get admission into any private schools, and I was finally admitted to an MCGM school in Grade 3.

I was always a studious student, avoiding extracurricular activities because I believed that only academics would help me become successful in my life and provide a better life for myself and my family. After Grade 7, I switched schools and enrolled in a low-income private school, where I continued to excel, consistently securing the first rank. Getting this first rank, along with the influence of my schoolteacher, persuaded me to pursue Science stream, believing that becoming a doctor was the right path for me as I was good with Science and Mathematics.

I enrolled in the science stream and completed my Grades 11 and 12 while also preparing for the NEET exam to enter medical school. During this time, however, I sometimes felt that the medical profession might not be for me. Still, I kept hearing about how it is a noble profession and that although it is tough, your future is secure once you succeed. I began to think my doubts were just temporary motivational issues, so I started listening to motivational stories and continued preparing. But eventually, I grew tired of relying on external motivation. After much thought, I made the difficult decision to stop pursuing medicine and discussed it with my parents.

It took me time to explain myself, to understand and accept this decision, as it meant letting go of a dream I had held for years – or perhaps, on further thought, one I had just been influenced into pursuing. This was the first time I asked myself, 'What next? What's next, Nikesh?'

Finding the answer to that question was not easy. I began exploring all the opportunities that came my way. During this discovery process, I was introduced to a Career Guidance session run by Antarang Foundation, where, for the first time, I spent time understanding my interests, strengths, and possible career options. I also learned about professional and interpersonal skills and how crucial they are in life.

After finishing the Career Guidance course, I heard about a business idea pitch competition organized by Udaan India Foundation, where I participated and, for the first time, understood the importance of mentorship. This was just the beginning, and at Udaan India Foundation, I started participating in other courses that helped me further develop my personal and professional skills. With this exposure, I found myself engaging in areas beyond academics, which I really enjoyed.

Along with all this, I was also pursuing a bachelor's degree in computer science, which I had enrolled in after attending my

Career Guidance sessions. I was eager to apply the new skills and knowledge I had gained in a real-world setting. I was particularly interested in joining the NGO sector or the start-up world, as I believed these environments would offer the most diverse learning opportunities in a short time.

To my surprise, I came across a career opportunity related to a course I had taken on design theory and design software. The role was in Vertical Communications, which was unfamiliar to me at the time. Initially, I felt unsure, but after reviewing the roles and responsibilities, I realised that my design experience would be highly relevant, and I felt more confident about stepping into this new space.

I began my journey in the NGO sector as a Communications intern at the same organisation where I attended the Career Guidance sessions. This experience opened up an entirely new world for me. While working there, I gained valuable insights into various departments and discovered that fundraising was something I was interested in. I eventually transitioned into my current role in fundraising, which I have come to enjoy deeply. In this role, I have the opportunity to connect with CSR heads and high-net-worth individuals and collaborate closely with the senior leadership team in my organisation.

Looking back, my journey has been nothing short of transformational. Every challenge, every choice, and every small victory has been woven together to shape the person I am today. That simple question, 'What next?' – once a fleeting thought – has now become the compass guiding my life. It's a question that propels me forward, reminding me that no matter where I stand, there's always more to learn, explore, and achieve. It's not just a question – it's a call to action, a reminder that our potential is limitless. In asking 'What next?' we open doors to growth, discovery, and boundless opportunities. And in that pursuit, we realise that the journey itself is where true fulfilment lies.

Regards,
Nikesh

MUSKANPREET'S STORY

Dear Reader,

I live in Mumbai, but my mother lives in Punjab. I have always loved poetry, dance, and music. Dancing is my true passion, but I also dream of becoming an investment banker.

When I was a child, my life was very happy. But as I grew into my teenage years, things started to change. I began to feel more and more sad. I became very emotional and would cry over small things. I would burst into tears if a friend didn't talk to me. I didn't understand why I felt this way. My studies started to suffer because I was always overthinking and felt mentally exhausted. Since childhood, it has been just my mother taking care of us, because my father had passed away.

When my mother moved to the village, I felt utterly lost. I didn't know who to share my feelings with. I wasn't close to my mother then, so I couldn't confide in her. This period was very hard for me because I felt incredibly lonely and like no one was there for me. During this time, YouTube became my safe place. I used to think that YouTube had answers to all my questions, so whenever I had a problem, I would ask YouTube. I always got good answers, and it made me feel less lonely. I learned a lot from YouTube, like about being more confident and expressing myself better. My English also improved because of YouTube, which helped me immensely in school and with talking with others. Over time, things began to get better.

I gradually started to open up to my mother and share everything with her. Slowly, she became my best friend. Now, I share everything with her and feel much better. Living alone taught me a lot about handling things on my own. The challenges I faced were tough, but I overcame them. Now, everything I do is for my mother because she has worked so hard to raise my sister and me on her own. Her struggles have been much greater than mine, and I feel that my own problems are small in comparison to hers. One day, I am determined to become an investment banker and fulfil all my mother's dreams.

Regards,
Muskanpreet

Nandini's Story

Dear Reader,

I'm a 12th-standard student pursuing a commerce degree, living in Mumbai with my loving family. I have grown up in a supportive and encouraging environment. My family and Udaan have always been my pillars of strength.

I aspire to become a Chartered Accountant (CA). My dreams are big, and I'm determined to achieve them. In my free time, I enjoy sketching and travelling, which help me unwind and broaden my horizons.

My journey so far has been a mix of hard work, learning, and growth. I'm proud of my perseverance and the progress I've made towards my goals. However, I've also faced challenges like balancing academics and hobbies and overcoming self-doubt.

Through my journey, I've learned the importance of staying focused, seeking guidance, and embracing new experiences. I'd love to learn more about time management, leadership, and creative problem-solving to enhance my skills.

As I continue on this path, I'm excited to see where my passions and dedication take me. I hope to inspire others to chase their dreams, just as I am doing.

Sincerely,

Nandini

Nandlal's Story

Dear Reader,

This is my story, which started eight years ago when I joined an NGO named Udaan. At that time, there were many difficulties in my life, and I didn't know what I would do next. Earlier, I was very afraid of expressing my views to anyone. I did not understand how to face my problems.

When I joined Udaan, changes gradually started taking place in my life. The people there were very supportive of me. They not only helped me in my studies but also showed me the direction in life. Most of all, they gave me confidence, which I had completely lacked.

With the help of this NGO, I not only got an education, but I also learned to stand on my own feet. I was given information about business, and gradually, I started my own small shop. Today, I am a successful businessman and have two shops named, 'Chandu Bookstore'.

This journey was not easy. There were many ups and downs, but Udaan never let me lose. It supported me in every difficult moment and taught me that accepting defeat is not an option.

When I look back, I am proud of how far I have come. My life has completely changed. I am now motivated not only for myself but also to help others.

Udaan has become an important part of my life, and I will always be grateful for their contribution.

Regards,
Nandlal

NEHA'S STORY

Dear Reader,

I am 18 years old and was born and brought up in Mumbai. I am pursuing a first year B Com course at R J College. Including me, there are six members in my family. My father is an auto driver, and my mother is a housewife.

When I was born, my father was not happy because he wanted his first child to be a son, as in my family, all of my uncles and aunts had their first child as a son, and my father was the only one who had a first child as a daughter. When I grew up and got to know this, it hit me really hard. That day, I decided that I would do everything to make my father feel proud.

Over time, he saw my hard work and potential and focused on me and is helping me fulfil my potential. My father always dreamed that we would all get a proper education to build a bright future. He wanted us to study in a private school. Private schools have expensive fees, which we could not easily afford. However, my father worked hard and enrolled us in a private school.

It wasn't always easy. I remember the times when the teacher would make me stand outside the class during exams, because my fees were not paid. Things became even more critical during the COVID lockdown, as my father lost his source of earnings. We went to our village for many months, and when we came back with pending loan amounts, our situation was dire.

I tried to focus on the only thing that was in my control – putting in my best effort and trying to excel at my studies. One of my teachers at Udaan, Amit Bhaiya, really motivated me and helped me to discover my potential. In my 10th Board Exams, thanks to his guidance and my hard work, I scored 81 per cent. Amit Bhaiya has been my guru, teaching me more than just about studies, and he once told me, 'The takers may eat better but the giver always sleeps better'.

I have a long way to go, but I know that I will continue working hard, not just for myself, but for my family, and to give something back to the society and community I come from.

Regards,
Neha

Nikita's Story

Dear Reader,

I'm introverted and find socialising difficult. Though I'm chatty with close friends and family, most people don't see the real me because I live in my own world. I can be a bit quirky with those I'm comfortable with. My life might seem quiet, but I find solace in my imagination as the real world can be harsh. I'm still figuring myself out, but I'm on a journey of self-discovery.

I've faced several challenges. Growing up, I was always shy and introverted, even around relatives. Making friends was tough, and in college, I learned that you don't always need to force friendships – being with yourself can be enough. I tend to overthink, making things even harder. When people ignore me or say something rude, I dwell on it and end up overthinking. I used to cry over small things, and I still get hurt easily.

Despite these challenges, I'm learning to overcome them. I'm working on not overthinking and living more in the present. Though it's tough, I'm gradually improving. I appreciate my few kind and supportive friends. I've accepted that not everyone has to like me, and that's okay. Even when I get hurt, I remind myself that life is too short to dwell on it for too long.

I'm often confused about my future. I like many things but don't feel like I'm really good at anything yet. I'm unsure about my career path or where I'm headed, and that uncertainty worries me. But more than anything, I want to be a kind person. That's the one thing I'm sure of, no matter what I end up doing.

One of my best qualities is my sensitivity, even though it can be challenging. I find joy in small things, which makes life a little brighter.

I come from a small, lower-middle-class family, and we live simply. My dreams reflect my love for simple joys. I want to visit places related to Radhakrishn, such as Thailand and South Korea, with my best friend. My favourite Thai actors inspire me, and I want to attend their events because they bring me happiness when I'm sad. In the future, I hope to live somewhere peaceful and quiet, away from crowds.

If given the chance, I would love to help street animals and elderly people in need. I would like to build shelters for animals, providing them with food and protection. I also want to help homeless and elderly people, offering them food and shelter because seeing them suffer breaks my heart.

I've learned to embrace my sensitivity and the happiness I find in small things. This is just the beginning of my journey; there's more to come as I grow older. I want to stay true to my childish nature and never lose that part of me. I'm thankful to Radha and Krishna for always being with me during my low times.

Regards,
Nikita

NISHA'S STORY

Hello Everyone,

In this city of dreams, I, too, have had big dreams. Right from childhood, I have tried to achieve them.

Making those dreams come true is not an easy path, and sometimes, one doesn't even know where to start. In a middle-class family like ours, the key is often education. Getting good marks in exams is seen as the way to get going on the journey to making one's dreams come true. However, I knew I wasn't as good at studies as some friends.

In 8th standard, I downloaded an app called Topper to try and improve my grades, but I deleted it within five minutes because it wasn't what I had hoped for. I thought I'd get help from my friends with my studies. The next day, someone called from Topper, offering a counselling session. A counsellor came and asked many questions about my studies, and I tried to answer them honestly, saying that I wanted to improve and give my best. I was conscious that my mother was there, and I wanted to show up in the best way possible. I was shocked when he rejected me after seeing my past report cards, writing in his report that I wasn't interested in studies.

I cried the whole night. Was I really not good enough? Did my efforts and dreams count for nothing? Was I nothing more than my past report cards? Was I condemned to let my family's dreams down?

That incident showed me a mirror, showing me that I could think what I wanted and say what I wanted, but unless I translated that into effort and results, it didn't matter. I started studying harder than I ever had, and then, over time, I was introduced to Udaan and Shilpa Ma'am. They taught me so much – the ability to dream big and learn and grow, that setbacks often show us the path forward, and that I should make myself capable so that people would offer me opportunities.

Marks are not everything in life, but the ability to translate dreams to action is, as is the confidence to stand in front of people and be oneself.

Regards
Nisha

OWAIS'S STORY

Dear Reader,

I am a 16-year-old boy from a middle-class family. I am writing to share my journey, aspirations, and the dreams that drive me forward. Every step I take is motivated by a deep desire to make my family proud and to carve out a unique place for myself in the world. Through my efforts and perseverance, I hope to achieve something special and bring a sense of fulfilment and joy to my family.

From a young age, I have harboured ambitious and diverse dreams. One of my primary goals is to become an influencer. In today's digital age, influencers have the power to impact and inspire people on a grand scale, and I am eager to be a part of that transformative world. I envision using social media platforms to share my passions, values, and experiences with a wide audience, hoping to connect with and motivate others along the way.

In addition to becoming an influencer, I have a strong desire to participate in the reality show, *Khatron ke Khiladi.* This show represents not only an opportunity to face thrilling challenges but also a chance to push my limits and demonstrate my resilience. The idea of conquering fears and embracing adventure excites me, and I believe that being part of such a high-energy environment would be both exhilarating and fulfilling.

Another significant aspiration of mine is to pursue singing. Music has always been an integral part of my life, and I have found solace and joy in expressing myself through songs. The prospect of sharing my voice and connecting with people through music is something that deeply motivates me. I am committed to honing my craft and exploring every opportunity that comes my way to achieve this dream.

Reflecting on my journey so far, I can say that it has been relatively simple but filled with its own set of challenges. I am proud of how I have navigated these challenges with determination and resilience. One of my strategies for overcoming difficulties has been to engage in self-reflection. I often talk to myself in front of the mirror, using this time to process my thoughts and address the obstacles I face. This practice has been instrumental in helping me stay focused and maintain a positive outlook.

During the most trying times, I have also relied on the support of my special ones – those who offer me guidance, encouragement, and comfort. Their presence in my life has been invaluable, and I am grateful for their unwavering support. Their belief in me has strengthened my resolve and inspired me to continue striving toward my goals.

In addition to my aspirations and personal growth, I have a keen interest in learning about reptiles. This fascination has led me to explore the world of these creatures and understand their behaviour and habitat. My curiosity about reptiles is just one example of how I seek to expand my knowledge and embrace new experiences.

In conclusion, my journey is a blend of personal growth, dreams, and passions. I am committed to pursuing my goals with dedication and resilience, always striving to make my family proud. I look forward to the opportunities that lie ahead and am excited about the future. Thank you for taking the time to read about my journey and aspirations.

Yours Truly,
Owais

Pooja's Story

Dear Reader,

I'm a Registered Nurse, currently working in a specialty hospital in the UAE.

Everyone has dreams, whether those dreams are big or small.

I wanted to go abroad for a job. I was not clear about where to go because I did not have much idea about opportunities, but I thought I had to go somewhere. I was not that interested in studies, but my brother and many other children had joined Udaan and they got a lot of benefits, so I thought that I could also get these benefits if I joined Udaan.

When I joined Udaan, I saw that the teachers put so much effort into giving us knowledge, and I began questioning myself. Why couldn't I put in effort, too? So, I started studying, and soon, the question arose: what would I do after the 12th standard?

I first wanted to become a nurse, but when I learned that the salary was very low, I gave up my dream of nursing. Then, my Didi at Udaan made me understand that nursing has a lot of scope, so I was admitted to a nursing college.

Nursing college fees were very high, but Udaan gave me scholarships every year. Going there made me feel like my dream could come true. Had Udaan not supported me financially, I don't know if I would have been able to study – there were multiple siblings in my family, and I don't know if Papa would have been able to support me in my studies. But today, because of Papa and Udaan, I have come outside India for a job and I feel very proud thinking that I have done something different in my life.

I am the first daughter in my family to work outside India, and every parent feels proud if their daughter works somewhere outside India.

My mother proudly tells everyone that her daughter works in Dubai. It feels so good when your parents are happy, and you are happy. All these dreams were fulfilled only because of Udaan.

Thank you so much, Udaan, for fulfilling this dream which every middle-class child sees.

Regards,
Pooja

Poonam's Story

Dear Reader,

I am from Mumbai, Maharashtra, and live at IIT Powai. My father is a painter, and my mother is a housewife. I have one elder brother, who is a Computer Engineer, and two younger sisters, who are both studying.

My goal is to get a government job in the healthcare industry.

I completed my education in SSC at Dyanmandir School in Powai. After completing my schooling, I was told by one of my schoolteachers, Ms Nagarkar, about Udaan. As a reward for my score of 81% at school, she helped me with the fee. Joining Udaan opened up many doors for me as I learned vital skills like spoken English and computer skills, which would prove very helpful in my professional life. Udaan has guided and driven me at every step on my path to success.

After my Higher Secondary Exams, I took the medical entrance exam because I wanted to work in the healthcare industry, but I couldn't score enough to get in there. I felt distraught and lost because I wanted to help my family financially. In desperate search of opportunity, I went to the Udaan office, where Mrs Malika introduced me to various short-term paramedical courses that could quickly equip me with skills that would open more doors for me. With financial support from Udaan, I enrolled in a one-and-a-half-year-long course in Radiography at Vivo Healthcare in Thane.

Following this, I completed a radiography internship at Nanavati hospital and secured a job as an X-ray technician at a hospital in Powai between 2020-2023. Then, I worked at a health medical centre in Gateway Plaza as a dental X-ray technician, and now I work at Nahar Medical Centre as an X-ray technician. I am still searching for more knowledge and future opportunities, so I am doing an Medical Laboratory Technology (MLT) internship, too.

My interest in MLT was born during the COVID pandemic when I noticed the RTPCR test, which was being performed by lab technicians. This got me interested in MLT, so I decided to get a degree in it while continuing my job. With Udaan's financial support, I was admitted to Premier College, Panvel.

The Pandemic was very challenging for me. I had to wear PPE kit, glasses, and face mask, as well as maintain hand hygiene. The patients were filled with anxiety, fear, and stress, but we worked to keep them calm and relaxed. I never lost hope, trust, and courage, trying to keep myself positive with hard work and patience. I did my best, and we overcame these obstacles.

I am proud that I'm a health worker; I never stepped back or left my job during the COVID-19 Pandemic.

I am trying hard to make my family's condition better.

Regards,
Poonam

Priyanka's Story

Dear Reader,

Growing up in a middle-class family of five, I always had dreams of doing something extraordinary. But like many others, I was clueless about how I'd achieve them. I was born and brought up in a small household where we depended on my father, the sole breadwinner. He worked hard to provide for all of us, ensuring we had everything we needed, though luxuries were rare. For a long time, I took life as it came, without realising the hard work and sacrifice that went into making sure our family kept moving forward.

I completed my education in a vernacular medium, which initially didn't feel like a limitation. But when I entered standard 11th and 12th, things took a sharp turn. Suddenly, I found myself struggling in ways I hadn't anticipated. As 11th and 12th standards were English medium, the language barrier was very real, and I struggled to keep up with the academic challenges I faced. It felt like I was starting from scratch. Everything was different, and it hit me hard. This was a turning point in my life – I could either sink under the pressure or fight to rise above it. I chose the latter. I started working on myself rigorously, especially focusing on improving my language skills. It wasn't easy, but I knew it was essential if I wanted to succeed.

In the midst of these personal battles, life dealt our family a significant blow. One day, my father fell seriously ill. With him unable to work, our family's income came to a standstill. Suddenly, we were facing financial instability on top of everything else. This was one of the toughest times for all of us. We had to make sacrifices and adjust to a new normal. Yet, through it all, I remained determined to complete my graduation.

After graduating, I was eager to start working to support my family and ease the financial burden. But when I asked my mother for permission, she told me something that stayed with me ever since. She said, 'Once you start working, your focus will shift to earning money, and you'll lose sight of your education. You'll get stuck in the cycle of making more and more, and that will make it harder to pursue further studies'. Her words hit me hard. For a while, I hesitated, but they gave me the clarity I needed.

Instead of rushing into work, I applied for post-graduation. Around the same time, I was also taking courses from the Udaan India Foundation. I worked hard and became one of their most dedicated students. My efforts were recognised by my Didis at Udaan, who were impressed with my progress and awarded me with an internship at Udaan. It was a moment of pride for me, as I got to know that my hard work was paying off.

Since then, I've been associated with Udaan and have recently been promoted. This achievement is significant, but it's not the end. I see it as the beginning of something much bigger. My journey has been filled with challenges, but I've promised myself that I will not give up. No matter what comes my way, I am determined to keep moving forward, with the belief that the best is yet to come.

Yours,

Priyanka

Radhakant's Story

Dear Reader,

My life has been shaped by the incredible individuals who have guided and supported me along the way. They have been my life's traffic lights, illuminating my path and showing me the way. They have shown me when to stop (red light), when to get ready (yellow light), and when to go full speed ahead and grab opportunities (green light).

Growing up in a small town before we moved to Mumbai, I was always drawn to the unknown, eager to explore the world beyond my familiar surroundings. When I first learned about Udaan eight years ago, my journey started with excitement, full of guidance and support. It was through Udaan that I began my transformation from an introvert to an extrovert.

I am a 22-year-old with a heart full of dreams and an insatiable curiosity. I grew up in a small chawl area, living with my nuclear family. Although I completed my studies up to the 7th grade at a municipal school due to financial constraints, I always had unwavering support from my family. Our neighbours connected us to the Sant Nirankari Mission, teaching me valuable lessons about respect, kindness, and contentment.

Udaan India Foundation was a turning point in my life. I joined Udaan after my elder brother enrolled, drawn by the promise of extra classes and a supportive learning environment. Despite my initial academic struggles, Udaan's affordable fees and dedicated teachers helped me overcome challenges and excel in my studies.

After completing my studies, I had the opportunity to work as a Supply Chain Intern for 12 months at General Mills India, thanks to Udaan. During my internship, I explored various aspects of supply chain management, interacted with people from different teams, and learned to use software tools like SAP and OMP.

With the invaluable support of my mentor and internship programme manager, I was able to navigate the internship effectively and gain valuable insights into the field of supply chain management. My mentors provided guidance, advice, and encouragement, helping me to improve my communication skills, boost my confidence, and overcome challenges.

My hard work and dedication during my internship, combined with the support of my mentor and programme manager, led to a permanent role as an Associate Supply Analyst for Raw Materials in Supply Chain. I've now been in this role for over a year and continue to learn and grow.

I'm proud of my journey from introversion to extroversion, from being an ordinary child in a chawl in Mumbai to working in a multinational, and all my learnings and achievements on the way. I have achieved this thanks to the support and encouragement of my mentors and friends at Udaan. Overcoming challenges like my initial academic struggles and self-doubt required perseverance and hard work. With my mentors' help, I developed my confidence, improved my communication skills, and achieved academic success.

I plan to continue my studies to stay competitive in today's world. I seek guidance and support from my mentors to navigate my career path and develop my soft skills. I aspire to grow professionally, becoming a leader who can make positive decisions for organisations and people. I want to be known as a supportive and encouraging mentor, helping others to achieve their goals. My dream is to spread happiness and be a source of inspiration for those around me.

My mentors have been the guiding lights in my journey, just like the traffic lights. Udaan India Foundation and my mentors have played a crucial role in shaping me into the person I am today. They have provided me with opportunities, support, and mentorship that have helped me grow and overcome challenges.

I am grateful for the unwavering support of my family and friends, who have always believed in me and encouraged me to pursue my dreams.

As I continue to grow and learn, I hope to pay it forward by mentoring others and helping them to reach their full potential. Remember, with the right guidance and determination, anything is possible.

Warm regards
Radhakant

RAJAN'S STORY

Dear Reader,

Hello everyone. I am working as a Staff Consultant at Oracle at present. My journey began in Uttar Pradesh, where I was born, but it was in Mumbai, where I grew up, that I found my footing. My father works as an auto driver, and my mother takes care of our family, which includes my elder sister, my younger brother, and me.

Growing up in a family with limited financial means taught me the value of hard work, and it's always been my dream to build something of my own – a business venture that I can call my own. But the journey to where I am today hasn't been easy. I'm proud of the tough choices I've made and the perseverance I've shown along the way. I know there's still so much to achieve, but here's the story of how I got to this point.

Up until grade three, my life was moving along predictably. That changed when I was introduced to Udaan, an organisation that became a turning point in my life. I had thought it might be just another school, but it turned out to be filled with opportunities and growth.

Here, I was exposed to things that opened new worlds for me, like computer courses, spoken English, and even robotics. I thrived in this environment, and for the first time, I felt truly confident in my abilities. By the time I reached my 10th standard, I had worked hard and scored well. But once again,

I found myself lost when it came to deciding on the next step. My family, with their limited education, couldn't guide me. Fortunately, Udaan came through once again. This time, the Didi who founded Udaan took me under her wing. She helped me explore my interests and decide on the path forward.

However, life at home was difficult. We were struggling financially, and I knew I had to contribute. So, after completing my 10th standard, I took my first job as a newspaper delivery boy. Waking up early and working before school was challenging, but it taught me valuable lessons in responsibility and perseverance.

I had completed my 10th standard from a Hindi-medium school and transitioning to 11th standard in an English-medium college was a harsh reality check. I struggled to understand basic concepts, not because I couldn't learn them but because I was still grappling with the language barrier. While my peers adapted quickly, I took three to four months to feel comfortable with English. By that time, many of the foundational concepts had already been taught.

My performance suffered in both 11th and 12th standard, but I refused to give up. I knew that with the proper focus and determination, I could catch up. After 12th, I made the difficult decision to take a gap year. I wanted to focus on improving my knowledge and preparing for engineering entrance exams. It was a risky move, and it wasn't easy. But with guidance from my Didi at Udaan and the support of my family, I gave it my all. During that year, I studied harder than ever before, revisiting everything I had struggled with in 11th and 12th.

When I finally took the engineering entrance exams, my efforts paid off. I secured a good rank and even earned a prestigious scholarship that was awarded to only two students in each branch of my college. It was a proud moment for me and a relief for my family, as it eased the financial strain.

Despite the scholarship, college life brought its own challenges. Engineering projects, books, and practical instruments required more money than my newspaper job could provide. So, I started working at Apsara Ice Cream Parlour. My routine: I delivered newspapers from 5 to 6 am, went home to freshen up, then attended college from 8 am to 5 pm. After that, I worked at the ice cream parlour from 7 pm to 1:30 am.

This routine lasted for two weeks, but soon, the lack of sleep began affecting my studies. Realising I couldn't continue like this, I decided to quit the newspaper job and focus solely on the ice cream parlour work. This is how I lived until my sixth semester, just before placement season began.

The COVID-19 pandemic brought unexpected challenges. When placements started, interviews were conducted online. I didn't have a laptop at the time, so I borrowed a friend's laptop for my first interview. Unfortunately, I couldn't clear the coding round, and it was a wake-up call for me.

I spoke to my mother, explaining that I needed a laptop to practice coding and prepare for interviews. Soon after, we bought a second-hand laptop, and I dove into preparation. Despite the effort, I faced rejection from eight to nine companies. But with each interview, I got a little closer to success, and soon, I was consistently surviving 3-4 rounds. These small victories kept me going.

After months of rejections, things started looking up. I finally cracked interviews with Cognizant, TCS, and Brillio. I was happy but still had my eyes set on something bigger. I applied for Oracle and, after clearing two rounds, I was anxiously waiting for the final HR interview results.

I'll never forget that moment. I was at Apsara Ice Cream when I received an email from my college with the Oracle selection list. My name was there. Overcome with joy, I called my mother to share the news, and I also informed the Udaan Didi, who responded with her signature phrase: 'Arey wah, fantastic se bhi fantastic!'

Today, as I work at Oracle, I reflect on my journey with pride. From a newspaper delivery boy to an Oracle consultant, every challenge I faced made me stronger. But this is only the beginning. I'm still dreaming of starting my own business to create opportunities for others like me.

If my story teaches anything, it's that no matter how tough the road, perseverance, and belief in yourself can take you to places you never imagined. My journey continues, and I'm excited to see where it leads.

Regards,
Rajan

RANJEET'S STORY

Dear Reader,

I'm a chef on a cruise ship, but it wasn't easy to get here. I come from a middle-class family in Mumbai, where dreaming big was a challenge.

My family's financial situation was not good, so I had to struggle a lot to achieve my dreams. However, I didn't give up and worked hard to fulfil my passion. I worked hard in hotels for 5 years, learning and growing as a chef. Then, I decided to take a big step and apply for a job on a cruise ship. I faced many problems while applying for a passport – I didn't have a birth certificate, and the police verification process was a hurdle. Sometimes, I felt like giving up, thinking that traveling abroad was not meant for me. Despite this, I didn't lose hope.

The next day, I tried again, requesting the police, and after 2-3 hours, they finally approved my file. Two days later, I received a text saying that my passport had been dispatched. I felt a sense of relief and peace. Even after that, there were many obstacles, but I didn't give up. I started attending interviews for jobs. I went to many places, but most required me to pay for the opportunities. As a middle-class person, I couldn't afford it. In spite of these financial issues and rejections, I kept attending interviews.

One day, I went for an interview with my candidate number being 842, a number I will always remember. I was selected in the first round, and after clearing the second round, I finally got the job. I was ready to take off! Finally, after a lot of hard work and patience, I had got the job! I was so happy and proud of myself. I started my career on the cruise ship, and it's been an amazing journey so far. I get to travel to different countries, meet people from different cultures, and learn new things every day.

I'm grateful for the journey that brought me here. I learned that if you work hard, believe in yourself, and never give up, you can achieve your dreams. I will be forever grateful to all my seniors and others who helped me on my beautiful journey.

I want to tell everyone not to give up and to believe in their dreams. Nothing is impossible if you work hard and believe in yourself.

Regards,
Ranjeet

RIDDHI'S STORY

Dear Reader,

Hello, mine is just another voice in a world full of stories, but my story is unique to me. I'm here to share my journey – a journey of mistakes, lessons, dreams and hopes for a better future.

I live with my small family, my sister and parents, in Mumbai, and I'm currently in my first year of college. Nothing has gone as expected, but I'm learning to go with the flow. When I first received this opportunity to share my story, I was confused about what to write. Then it hit me – why not share my life's mistakes, lessons, and the change I wish to see in the world? Perhaps others would relate.

Before 10th grade, life was stable. Everything changed after that, and many experiences shaped me, as I learned from my mistakes. One of my biggest mistakes was tying my happiness to others' opinions. Seeking approval made me lose myself and left me feeling unworthy. I struggled with saying 'no', which led people to take advantage of me.

Over time, I developed stress and anxiety as I realised that I was living a life that wasn't truly mine. Later, I developed a habit of reading, and self-help books and videos helped me learn self-validation and set boundaries. I want others like me to know that the only opinion about yourself that truly matters is your own. Fear of judgment caused me to miss many opportunities. I remember being afraid to raise my hand in class even when

I knew the answer, thinking people would think I was stupid. This fear also stopped me from trying new things, but later, I started to try things without worrying about failure. Eventually, I realised no one really cares as much as I thought – they're busy with their own lives. I also learned that we have to give ourselves permission to fail, or else we'll never grow.

College was very different. As an introvert, I struggled with socialising and having conversations, often feeling anxious around my peers. I spent a lot of time alone, which helped me better understand myself. I learned that making friends is not a necessity and that friendships should come naturally, not out of a need to fill a void. Now, I find happiness within myself.

There are many incidents that have changed the way I think. I have a strong urge to share this one incident that really made me question our society's mindset. During a group project, two classmates with great ideas were sidelined in our class because they weren't confident in English. They were from vernacular backgrounds and were given less significant roles, even though they had much to contribute. In every sector, whether it is education, sports, corporate, or the film industry, we all start to judge people by what they can or cannot do based on their physical appearance, gender, disability, etc, which is wrong. I want this to change in society so that every individual can get an 'Equal Opportunity'. It's unfair not to give everyone an equal chance to prove themselves, and for society's progress, this must change.

This was my journey that shaped me into a more self-aware and confident individual, and I hope reading it has inspired you, too.

Regards
Riddhi

Rinki's Story

Hello,

I was the kind of girl who felt very bad when anyone used to talk to me in a raised voice. In fact, I would feel so bad that I would start crying. But as I grew up, I changed, and eventually, what others said stopped mattering to me.

They say that everyone has some childhood dream or the other. I, too, had a dream- to become a teacher. This dream was born when I saw the teachers at Udaan, with their soft hearts and great way of teaching, and I started hearing a voice inside me telling me I would become like them one day.

My dream wasn't like dreams usually are. Most people's dreams keep changing, but mine did not.

When I passed the 9th standard, I suddenly got to know about the dreams my father had about my brother, about him becoming successful and bringing glory to my father's name. I also learned that my father had not had any such thoughts about me, which hurt me and motivated me to become the one to bring happiness to my father before my brother did.

That is when I made the decision to become an IPS officer. I didn't forget my original dream, but it became plan B. After 12th standard, I thought I would conduct tuition classes at home while preparing for UPSC. Now, my 12th standard is going on. When it is over, I can start fulfilling my dreams. For now, my goal is to get a good percentage in 12th standard.

Regards,
Rinki

REETI'S STORY

Dear Reader,

I grew up in Mumbai and am currently in college. I come from a middle-class family of seven members. We are two brothers and two sisters, and my elder sister is special, needing extra care and support. Everyone is working in our family except for my mother and me.

I have a dream of becoming a journalist. In the future, I want to interview famous political figures and make a positive impact through journalism. Before choosing journalism as a career, I did a lot of research. I wanted to know what I needed to study, which colleges offered journalism, and how to build a path toward this profession. I even registered on platforms like Shiksha.com to gather information. Journalism is my way of helping the community and contributing to a better Bharat.

However, the journey has not been easy. I have faced many obstacles both at home and in my studies. When I started my degree, I heard negative comments about journalism – people said it had no future, that I would lose my job, and that I needed to increase my connections. At first, I was confused because I didn't understand what 'connections' meant in this context. But I reached out to speakers who were journalists, and with their guidance, I began working on myself and preparing for my career.

One of the biggest challenges for me has been overcoming my laziness and learning to study in English despite being more comfortable with Hindi. During COVID-19, my studies suffered, and I got lower marks, but I kept pushing myself to improve. I am proud of the fact that I've changed – I used to make excuses and run from opportunities, but now I am more focused and determined.

Despite this progress, I still struggle with stage fright. I have given multiple presentations, but each time feels like the first, and I still get nervous. I know I need to overcome this fear if I want to succeed in journalism. I also want to learn techniques to help me stay focused and on the right path, as this will be crucial in reaching my goals.

Thank you for reading my story. I am working hard every day to become a better version of myself and to make my dream of becoming a journalist come true.

Regards,
Reeti

Roshani's Story

Dear Reader,

Everything is possible in this world if our intentions are firm. I have experienced this in my own life!

Earlier, I thought that dreams were only imaginary things in our minds. Then came the day when we came to know about Udaan. As soon as we heard about Udaan, we started feeling like flying, that our dreams could come true. That first day when we sat in the yellow bus was a different kind of happiness, because before this we had never gone to school by bus, we often went on foot. That was the first day when we got down from the bus and reached Gopal Sharma School where Udaan classes were held. After reaching there, we came to know that schools could also be like this too, because we had only seen small schools we could go to earlier, as Papa had a small vegetable stall, and his earnings had to support me and my sister.

I still remember that day when the Didi at Udaan smilingly told me the meaning of dreams. That day I understood the real meaning of dreams. That day I also came to know that all our dreams can come true if we have the courage to pursue them. And I also understood that those who have the courage to dream can conquer the whole world. And then began the race to fulfil the dreams.

But it is not that easy. The struggle was about to begin. One afternoon, Papa came to know that Grandfather's health was very bad. We went to the village to meet him. It felt very good to go to the village, because I had never seen a village before. It showed me many new things that we probably did not even know about. The fields, the well, and many other things. We started preparing to go back to Mumbai and then Dadaji and Papa said that we would never go back to Mumbai and now we would always stay in the village.

I thought it was a joke, but then 15 days became 30 days and my high school exam which was to be held in Mumbai also passed. All these things kept breaking me from inside because just a few days back I had come to know about dreams and after a few days I had to leave my studies.

This sorrow came out like a fever inside me and I had to live with it for many days. I was completely broken. Now there was neither any dream nor any education because education is that one factor that can turn dreams into reality. After a few days, my fever was cured, and I started feeling a little better. Then I told Papa that I wanted to study. Papa agreed but Papa and I were well aware of our financial situation. At that time, Papa did not have enough money to get me admitted in a good school. But Papa also wanted me to study. Then Papa and Mummy sold their wedding gifts and got me admitted to a school. Now the worry of how to pay the fees for books and copies started bothering me. Then Papa went to Prayagraj and started doing labour work so that I could go to school. Finally, I went to school but there also many problems started coming up because I was brought up in Mumbai since childhood. I passed my high school examination with good marks – in fact, the highest any girl had ever got in my village.

Before me, no girl in my village had taken science, but I wanted to pursue further studies in science only. My grandfather and uncle said I had studied enough, and that I should do a social studies course. After all, after marrying, all I'd have to do is cook and bring up children. But I remembered Mamta Didi's words that your dream will be fulfilled only if you pursue it, and I told everyone that I will study science only. I passed my intermediate with very good marks, after fighting everyone, but the dreams were getting bigger now and there was a desire to complete them because the situation at home was also getting serious. Everyone said that I had completed my intermediate, and now I should get married, and my marriage was soon fixed.

I was to be married to someone because he was from a rich family and there was no demand for dowry. At that time, I did not even know what was happening to me. The date of marriage was also fixed and soon came. The elders of my village and my relatives all went to the boy's house to perform the wedding. Seeing the boy, who seemed to have some mental health issues, my uncle was very angry. Maybe he felt pity for me or my fate.

After coming home, he clearly said that this marriage would not happen, and my uncle took me to his house. The marriage was broken, but people started talking about all kinds of things. I ignored all this, and I did not give up and decided to do my BSc. My college was very far from my house, so I had to stay at my aunt's house. I went to college cycling 16 km very day.

While doing my BSc, I also filled the application form to join the police without telling anyone. By then I had completed my BSc degree and came back to my home. In the meanwhile, my marriage was fixed to a teacher. I had taken admission for my MSc degree and was reconciled to getting married. However, a few days before marriage, the boy's side demanded a Royal Enfield motorcycle which was beyond the reach of my family. Once again, my marriage broke.

Now, our society completely believed that there was something lacking in me and that is why two marriages had been broken. The atmosphere at home became like mourning but I still did not give up and passed the physical examination of Uttar Pradesh police on the same date.

Now, my marriage was fixed for the third time because the boy liked me. Things were much smoother this time. After two months of marriage, I got a call from Uttar Pradesh Police for their medical test. I don't know about society but the person I was married to supported me completely and my in-laws also supported me a lot, and finally, I was selected for Uttar Pradesh Police. I also completed my M Sc in Mathematics and even today I am studying. I have two small children, and I am also doing my job.

Because I never gave up. Nothing is impossible. Whatever you can think, you can do it. Whatever you do, do it with all your heart. Work makes the impossible possible.

Roshani

Rupa's Story

I was born into a life where dreams were luxuries, and hope was a fragile thing. My father was a skilled carpenter, devoted but stretched thin, working hard to provide for his family of six. I had three younger siblings, and though my parents gave me they could, the reality was that there was only so much to go around. From a young age, I learned to tuck away my own needs, my quiet dreams of a brighter future, understanding that my family could only do so much. I rarely voiced my ambitions, but deep within me, there was a fierce determination that refused to be snuffed out.

Attending a government school, I faced the realities of limited resources, crowded classrooms, and a constant, unspoken battle to simply keep up. My classmates saw a quiet, gentle girl who was diligent in my studies. But what no one saw was the silent war I fought each day, an internal struggle between my ambition and the reality of my situation. My teachers never knew how hard it was for me to study by the faint glow of a lamp late into the night, or how often I suppressed myr own dreams to make space for my siblings' needs. Beneath my calm surface was a quiet storm – a girl who wanted more, who knew I was meant for more, but who also bore the weight of responsibility.

In the midst of this struggle, Udaan India Foundation entered my life. Udaan wasn't just an NGO; they were a miracle I hadn't dared to pray for. They became my unwavering support system, the lifeline I didn't even know I needed. Udaan provided me with textbooks, extra tutoring, and, more importantly, mentors who looked at me and saw my potential. They saw my quiet strength, the untapped power of my resolve, and they nurtured it, helping me realise that I could dream, that I deserved to dream.

Every time I stumbled, every time my spirit waned under the weight of my inner battles, Udaan was there. They didn't just offer me academic support; they became my emotional anchor. When I doubted herself, they reminded me of the light I carried within. When I felt the strain of balancing family and education, they encouraged me to keep going, to believe in myself. They taught me that I was allowed to want more from life, that my calm, unassuming nature was the armour of a warrior, and that the struggles I faced were forging me into someone remarkable.

By the time I reached my final year, I was no longer the quiet girl simply enduring life. I was a force, a girl who had turned every setback into strength. And when she was named Best Student of 2018 in my school, it was more than an award. It was a culmination of every sacrifice I had made, every hour I had spent fighting my own doubts, every quiet battle Udaan had helped me win. They knew the story behind my smile, the countless silent battles that had led to that victory.

Today, I am working in a respected multinational company, fulfilling a dream that once seemed impossible. My colleagues see a calm, competent professional, but only I know the journey that led me here; the years of hidden struggles, the unspoken sacrifices, and the moments I almost gave up. I remember every time I felt lost and how Udaan lifted me, piece by piece, until I was ready to rise on her own.

My story is a testament to the power of quiet strength and relentless determination. I fought a war no one saw, and I won.

And now, I carry on her journey, a reminder of what it means to have people believe in you, to have a hand pulling you up when the world feels heavy. Calm on the surface, a warrior within, I have learned that all it takes to change a life is the gift of someone who believes in you.

This is my story.

Rupa

SACHIN'S STORY

Dear Reader,

I am from Uttar Pradesh. My father has a small clothes shop, and my mother is a housewife.

When I completed my 3rd standard, I came to Mumbai with my father. By then, I had become accustomed to seeing the open sky, riverbanks, and lush green fields, so this was a significant change for me. I got admission to a BMC school, but I missed the open air of my village, so I would run away from my school during breaks and come back home.

However, fate had something interesting in store for me. I got admission to Udaan, which was the turning point of my life. Along with studies, Udaan conducted many extracurricular activities and events, which removed my fear of the crowds and skyscrapers of Mumbai. Successful people used to come to Udaan to speak about their journeys, which inspired me to start dreaming big myself.

I worked harder at school and got very good marks in 10th standard.

However, I did not know what to do next. At that time, my Udaan Didi guided me through the storm. She was more worried than me about my admission to an engineering college. Three of my friends were also like me. We all wanted to become engineers but did not know how. We used to trouble our Udaan Didi by asking her all our questions. She named the four of us 'Four

Mosquitoes' because she was very stressed about our careers. Today, all four of us are software engineers at top MNCs, and it is only because of our Udaan Didi.

When I met Dr Annoottam Ghosh Sir in 12th standard, and he became my mentor, it was the second turning point of my life. After meeting him, I started finding solutions to almost all my life's problems, from engineering projects to problems in daily life. That's why I tell my friends that I was very lucky to have had him as my mentor.

In the second year of my degree course, I started two startups. They did not work, but I learnt a lot from this experience and made many good friends.

This is my story so far, and I have one piece of advice for my readers: Never think of the destination. Never define goals. Life is all about the ride, not the destination. Your destinations are already destined. No matter how hard you try or pretend to try, you just can't do anything about it. It's all about the ride. Never worry and enjoy the ride. Enjoy if someone else rides along with you. Enjoy if you are alone. Just enjoy and live your life.

Regards,
Sachin

SADIYA'S STORY

Dear Reader,

As a child, I was incredibly smart and curious. My parents took me to get admission to junior KG, but the school authorities were impressed by my advanced knowledge and selected me for senior KG instead. Thus, I felt proud and confident at the start of my educational journey.

Initially, I excelled in my studies and was known for being one of the smartest kids in my class. However, as time passed, my grades began to slip, and I struggled to keep up. Despite this, I discovered my creative side and excelled in dancing, drawing, and art. These activities brought me joy and helped me express myself.

Growing up, I was an introverted child, rarely speaking up or socialising with my classmates. I had no friends and felt lonely, often wondering why others couldn't understand me. I thought they were better than me, which made me hesitant to participate in class or join extracurricular activities.

In the 3rd standard, a new teacher joined our class, and I found her intimidating. She seemed strict and demanding, and I feared she would ask me questions I couldn't answer. I remained quiet, observing my classmates and avoiding eye contact with the teacher.

One day, our teacher announced the annual day celebrations and asked me who wanted to participate in the dance competition. I wanted to join, but my self-doubt held me back. I thought, 'What if I'm not good enough? What if I embarrass myself?' Still, I tried to participate and did. My ma'am thought I would not be able to do well.

I decided to take the plunge. To everyone's surprise, I performed well, and my dance skills earned me recognition at school. From then on, people knew me as the 'dance girl', and I gained confidence.

As I progressed through school, I continued to excel in drawing and art. I won a drawing competition, which made me famous in school. My artwork adorned the school's noticeboards, and I felt proud.

However, my parents didn't consider art a viable career path. They wanted me to focus on academics and pursue a more 'stable' profession. I tried to convince them otherwise, but they remained skeptical.

Around this time, in 6th standard, I joined the Scouts and Guides, and threw myself into the activities, learning valuable skills and teamwork. Soon, it became my dream to complete all five stages of it – Pratham Sopan, Dwitiya Sopan, Tritiya Sopan, Rajyapuraskar and Rashtrapati. I completed the first three stages at school.

For Rajyapuraskar, though, I had to go to Pune because it was a little high-level exam.

A few days before I went to Pune, I developed a fever. Still, I wanted to complete the Rajyapuraskar trial. On the first day, though, my condition became very serious. I needed to go to the doctor. My ma'am took me there, and then I had to go back home. I was disheartened but intended to take the exam again. However, the lockdown came, and because of that, I couldn't take the exam again.

The lockdown, though, was an opportunity to immerse myself in a new passion: fashion designing. I wanted to study it, but my parents discouraged me. They said it had no scope. They convinced me to join BBI (Bachelor of Banking and Insurance) instead.

My parents then suggested I take up training for joining the cabin crew in planes, thinking it would be a good career path. I got interested, too, but after I completed the training, they changed their minds. They said working as part of a cabin crew wouldn't be suitable and that I should consider a bank job instead.

Now, I'm torn between fashion design and work as part of a cabin crew. I love the aviation industry, but my passion for fashion design remains strong. I'm unsure which path to choose.

I've come a long way from being a shy child to discovering my passions. I've faced challenges, overcome self-doubt, and explored my interests. But the question lingers: what should I do?

Regards,
Sadiya

SAHIL'S STORY

Dear reader,

I still remember the day my grades started slipping in school. You won't believe the struggles I faced at school! It was like my life was a never-ending test match, and I was always on the verge of getting bowled out! I was just a kid trying to figure out my place in the world, but it felt like the whole world was stacked against me.

My parents were always after me about something, my grades were never good enough, and to top it all off, I was obsessed with Cricket – a sport my parents didn't even want me to play. They'd say, 'Focus on your studies, forget about Cricket!' But I couldn't help it – I was hooked! I'd watch matches all day, practice my shots in the backyard, and even dream about making a partnership of 200 runs with Virat Kohli, scoring centuries. But, as I grew older, I realised that my love for Cricket wasn't just about the game – it was about the sense of belonging and purpose it gave me. And when my parents refused to support me, it felt like they were taking away a part of me. I felt lost and alone, like I was wandering through life without a map. But I didn't let it get me down. I found other ways to stay involved in the game, like playing with friends, watching videos, and even commentating at local matches! Slowly but surely, I started to realise that life was bigger than just Cricket.

However, the setbacks kept coming. We couldn't afford coaching fees, so I never got the chance to hone my skills properly. It was like I was stuck in a perpetual state of 'what ifs?' What if I had the training? What if I had the support? What if I had the chance to pursue my dreams? But, as I look back, I realise that those setbacks taught me valuable lessons. I learned to channel my energy into other areas, like academics and personal growth, which ultimately shaped me into the person I am today.

I realised that life is unpredictable, and our plans often get derailed. But it's in those moments of uncertainty that we discover our true strength. We must learn to embrace the twists and turns and find ways to overcome obstacles. Life is like a Cricket match – sometimes you're on top, and sometimes you're getting hit for a six! But it's how we respond to those ups and downs that define us.

So, my story is not just about Cricket or setbacks – it's about finding purpose in the face of adversity and transforming our passions into something meaningful. Remember, every setback is an opportunity to rediscover ourselves and emerge stronger, wiser, and more vibrant than before. That's the message I take away from my journey, and I hope you can relate to it, too.

Regards,

Sahil

SANDEEP'S STORY

Dear readers,

I am an ordinary boy trying to make his mark. I was born in the Uttar Pradesh, in the district of Bhadohi. I am the fourth surviving child of my parents. People were happy at my birth. When I was four, my family brought me to Mumbai. Being away from my mother made me emotionally stronger at an early age. I started my academics at a municipal school in Powai. Although I was an average student, I had a keen interest in being noticed by the teachers. One of our Pandits said I would become a rich and famous person, so I started feeling special at an early age. Teachers used to think that I was a good student. I surrounded myself with better mentors and Gurus. Being surrounded by Gurus allowed me to have better morals and be eager to grow as a good human.

I had a great friend's circle. They were older than me and helped me grow. My friends and I had an age gap of 3-7 years, so they showed me the real world and prepared me for the years ahead. School friends are always special. I became more of an extrovert with age and started enjoying academics and school more. At the age of nine, I got the chance to join Udaan, thanks to my Didi from there, who is the angel of my life. Udaan has had a major influence on my life. I was in 4th standard when I joined Udaan. Udaan has played a vital role in shaping many lives, including mine. We got exposure and opportunities to experience things we could not have even imagined, and I learned many skills there, including things that would guide me for life, such as morals, values, and etiquette.

I passed 10th grade with good marks and got admission into the science stream. I tried to get admission into MBBS (Bachelor of Medicine and Surgery) but got BHMS (Bachelor of Homeopathy Medicine and Surgery). I felt like life had given me a tight slap. It was the biggest setback I have had in my life to date. But God had a different plan for me. I started working in a call centre in Powai. Further, Udaan gave me an opportunity to be a programme intern. There, I learned interpersonal skills. Next, I got admission to a pharmacy course. Pharma is perfect for me, as it allows me to apply my best skills, and I find it interesting. I got admitted into a Pharma College in Bangalore. My parents were very concerned about me, my accommodation, and my studies, as I had never lived alone in a different State.

Udaan helped me a lot through its Scholarship Programme. I got a diploma in Pharma easily and was convinced that I could do it well, so I decided to pursue a career in that field. The curriculum of B. Pharma (Bachelors of Pharmacy) was a bit tough, though. The driving force and motivation was my Udaan Didi, who said, 'Just keep the focus and the rest will fall into place'. This statement became my mantra. She had told me, 'Education can change anything', and I learned how true that statement is.

I was the first person in my family to leave home for education. Everything was a new experience and challenge. My father, however, believed in me. He is the strongest pillar of my life. Once, he lost his job and was not able to deliver the academic fees on time due to low financial savings. It was a hard test for us. I used to work part-time in a retail medical store in Bangalore and had to use this to pay my accommodation expenses for a few months. Still, I was unable to pay my college fees fully. It was a great survival lesson, but after some time I lost my patience.

One day, my college gave us a notice that without paying academic fees, we wouldn't be allowed to write the exams. Despairing, I came to Mumbai for a week and asked for financial help from my Udaan Didi. Without hesitation, she asked for my bank account details. I received the money the same day in the evening. I filled out the exam form and passed it with a good CGPA. I am very thankful to all those who helped me in that hard time. They all are and will be close to my heart.

Then came the tragic COVID-19 pandemic. I was part of the first human trial batch of the Covaxin antivirus vial in our college. I worked with Pharmeasy (the online pharmacy) during the second lockdown. I had a great time working and learning with them. After some time, I left Pharmeasy to focus more on academics and got a distinction in the final semester exam. After graduation, I thought of going for a master's degree. However, after much thought, I decided I did not want to get into more academics and wanted real-world experience. I worked with a diagnostics-based company for 6 months. I had always wanted to have something of my own, so I made a business plan within days.

I had almost no savings, so I had to take 1 lakh in cash as a gold loan at 2% interest on my mother's gold jewellery. I had a gut feeling I could run a business, so we took the risk to set up a Retail Pharma Store called 'Mamta Medical' in Powai, Mumbai. The early days were tough for the business, but we were tougher. People did not believe in us – my relatives kept questioning my decision to start the business, and no one invested in it for a long time. People said that my refusal to give up resulted from ego, but I told them I was driven by self-respect and pride in my work. Within one-and-a-half years, we had made a profitable bootstrap business.

My current position in life – whatever success I have achieved, and my aspirations for the future- are thanks to those who have uplifted me throughout my life, such as my family and the Udaan India Foundation.

Thank you, and I love you all.

Regards,
Sandeep

Sanjay's Story

Dear reader,

I have completed my Bachelor's in Engineering with a focus on Electronics and Computer Science. I often see my life as a maze, similar to the movie Maze Runner. In the movie, the characters navigate through a constantly changing and complex maze, overcoming obstacles and solving problems to find their way out. That's how I feel about my own journey – always facing new challenges, learning from them, and moving forward like a maze runner.

Sometimes, I look at the opportunities students have these days and feel that we were not given enough opportunities. It feels like advancements and opportunities only came after we left school. When I was about to complete my diploma, COVID-19 hit, and we went into lockdown. We missed out on practical learning experiences. After that, I enrolled in my Bachelor's programme, but we had almost a year of online classes. Although the placement stats were good, by the time we were about to graduate, a recession hit. It felt like companies hired people before and after our batch, but not us. I know I'm complaining, but it does feel like that sometimes.

However, life wasn't just about studying. We had fun, too. One memory that stands out is from my diploma days when our classes were in the basement. One day, while we were moving between labs, some construction was going on, and the area was dimly lit. My friend and I decided to play a prank on another friend by hiding and waiting to scare them. We heard footsteps approaching and were ready to jump out when we yelled, 'Bhaoww!' To our shock, it wasn't our friend but the college trustee! We froze in embarrassment. The clerk saw us and reported us to the principal, and we got punished. Later, we learned the trustee had a heart condition. It was funny in hindsight but also a bit dangerous!

Through everything that's happened in my life, I've learned a lot. From the recession, I learned how to improve my skills and create better opportunities for myself. I wasn't a top student and passed my SSC in second class. My dream was to become an engineer, but with low marks, getting into a good science college was tough. That's when Udaan and Mamta Didi helped me choose the right stream and achieve my goal. With their support and dedication, I completed my engineering with a CGPA of 7.5.

It's a journey of persistence, growth, and never giving up, no matter how difficult the path might seem.

My journey has had its ups and downs, but each step has been a lesson in growth, resilience, and finding my way through the maze.

Regards,
Sanjay

SARITA'S STORY

Dear Reader,

I am a 20-year-old girl from a small town with big dreams that touch the sky.

After my family moved to Mumbai when I was young, I grew up in a small chawl area, living with my happy family. I have always had my family's support. When I was young, our neighbours connected us to the Sant Nirankari Mission, teaching me valuable lessons about respect, kindness, and contentment. Until 7th grade, I was studying at a municipal school.

Then, connecting with the Udaan India Foundation changed my life. My elder brothers enrolled at Udaan, and I joined them since they said it was a helpful learning atmosphere. Despite my early difficulties in the classroom, Udaan's reasonable tuition and committed faculty helped me overcome obstacles and succeed in my studies.

After completing my studies, Udaan provided me with the opportunity of an internship as an assistant teacher in a school. One day, my Udaan Didi came to my classroom and told me that she had observed a great teacher's quality in my personality. Thinking about that day makes me realise that sometimes, we don't know what to do in our lives, but small things like one person's compliments can turn our lives into beautiful journeys. She also suggested that I enrol in one of the best colleges for Teacher Training – Bombay Teacher's Training

College, Colaba – and promised to give the financial support to complete all of my studies. I completed my teacher's training there and am blessed to have her financial and emotional support all the time.

After that, I got an offer to work as a full-time class teacher of Sr KG in a Government School. I am very thankful to my parents, my brothers, and all the teachers who have guided and supported me in achieving the career goals of my life.

I wish to give back as I develop and learn more by mentoring and assisting others in realising their full potential.

Regards,

Sarita

Shalini's Story

At times it's better to have no plans!

Hi folks,

I am a girl who has always had unexpected things happen in her life, to which she would have said, 'no'. My career journey was not as predicted, but I appreciate that whatever path the universe has chosen for me is the best one. At times, it's better to accept whatever comes your way and appreciate the magic of life.

By God's grace, I am a Chartered Accountant (CA), the first CA in my whole family. I work at an MNC as a Senior Specialist. I am at a very early stage of my working career. As far as my family is concerned, there are my parents and four siblings. My dad is an auto driver, and my mother is a homemaker. Despite facing financial problems, my parents have always encouraged us to study because they think that as they didn't get the chance to study, their children should get that opportunity. My parents are proud that their daughter is a CA.

It was 2010 when I, with my Udaan Didi's advice, decided to join a CA course considering my aptitude test results. After deciding that I would pursue CA, I had to choose Commerce. Although I had always wanted to be an engineer, somehow, with difficulty, I convinced myself that maybe I was not meant to do engineering. After completing grade 12, my CA studies started. I got exactly 50% in my CPT results. I was actually expecting less, so I was like, *'Jitna difficult main ye course ko samjh rahi thi utna difficult nahi hai'*. That was silly me, a 12th-grade pass, satisfied with poor results.

When I started IPCC, I realised the syllabus was quite humongous and difficult, but I thought, *'ek level aage jaa rahe hai toh thoda muskil toh hoga'*. I completed my classes and wrote my first attempt in May 2013. I couldn't crack it on my first attempt as my preparation was not up to the mark. It takes immense courage and determination to finish something which you have. Earlier, I was only thinking of clearing my CA exams, but after a number of attempts, I realised that it's more about me knowing my capability of becoming a CA.

There was a lot of discouragement to continue attempting as I had already made multiple attempts, so people around me suggested I do a job and study something else, such as an MBA or something. But I am quite stubborn when trying to get something, as I know if you can't take charge of your own life, then nobody, absolutely nobody, will do anything for you.

In this phase of failure in my journey, I was introduced to my mentor who held my hand and had faith in me. He was the only one who believed in me throughout my journey of being CA.

In 2016, I had cleared my IPCC papers in my seventh attempt. After this, I started my articleship in a mid-sized firm, which lasted three years. When COVID arrived, the whole world was affected, and my life slowed down too. There was now hope in everyone's eyes that I could be a CA, due to my success in the last few years. In May 2022, I cleared all the papers and became CA. That was the most memorable year for me.

Today, I am a CA, a law graduate and a Master's in Commerce. The only thing I understood from my journey was when you try to achieve something and put in all your efforts, even the Universe will help you achieve it.

Always believe in yourself and manifest the things that you want in your life. Always be hard-working and determined.

I quite often say that my name has been given by my parents, but the prefix that I hold (CA) is a lifetime gift to myself. I hope my story has encouraged you to achieve what you really want in your life. At times, accept and let the Universe take charge of your life. Trust me, you won't regret it.

Yours,
Shalini

SHIVAM'S STORY

Dear Reader,

In my family, there are four of us, my father is an auto driver, my mother is a homemaker, and my sister works at TCS. Their support has been my biggest source of strength throughout my journey.

Like many from small towns who moved to Mumbai, my journey started in a simple government school. Those ten years of schooling were filled with struggles, such as limited resources and an abundance of distractions. But despite the challenges, I was determined to make something of myself. I pushed through and scored 72% in my SSC exams, marking the first major milestone in my academic journey.

However, things weren't always smooth. During my time in a BMC school, especially in 8th and 9th grade, I fell into bad company. I started bunking classes, spending time with the wrong crowd, and stopped paying attention to my studies. There were times when I scored just 1 or 2 marks in my exams. It was a difficult phase, and I wasn't sure where I was headed. But even in those tough times, my family stood by me, and their belief in me played a huge role in helping me turn my life around.

After completing my SSC schooling, I faced a common dilemma: what to do next? My initial interest was in Science, but financial issues forced me to choose Commerce instead. At first, I felt it was a setback, but with guidance from the right people,

I began to embrace Commerce as an opportunity. I worked hard and managed to score 82% in my 12th-grade exams. This achievement filled me and my family with pride.

Once I finished 12th, another challenge emerged. Like many others, I had the goal of becoming a Chartered Accountant (CA). In our society, being a CA brings a lot of respect, and that societal pressure influenced my decision. Deep down, though, I was always drawn towards marketing and sales. My interest lay there, but I couldn't shake off the desire for the respect that came with being a CA. It was a confusing phase, not knowing which path to follow.

That's when my friends introduced me to Udaan, a career guidance programme. Udaan changed everything. It helped me realise what I was truly passionate about and what skills I needed to succeed. I learned essential skills like communication, English proficiency, computer literacy, and the importance of confidence in a professional setting. Udaan gave me the clarity I needed to choose a path aligned with my strengths and interests.

During the pandemic, when I was in my second year of college, I got the opportunity to intern at BYJU'S. It was my first real-world experience in the corporate world. I worked hard, and within a short period of time, I became the top performer in the pan-India team I was a part of. This recognition led BYJU'S to offer me a full-time job, and within six months, I was promoted to lead the team. It was a huge achievement, but as life teaches us, not all successes are permanent.

After some time, BYJU'S started facing a downturn, and I had to make another tough decision. In the end, I didn't let the situation discourage me and chose to apply to new companies, looking for the right opportunity. That's when I landed a position at OYO Weddingz.in as a Business Development Manager. It came with a decent package, but more importantly, it felt like the right place for me.

Life has its ups and downs. It's easy to feel lost, but those who push through, adapt, and keep moving forward are the ones who succeed. Every challenge I faced, whether it was the confusion after 12th grade, the downfall of BYJU'S, or finding the right career path, prepared me for the next step.

Today, I'm working in a field I'm passionate about – marketing and sales. My journey from a confused student in a government school to a successful Business Development Manager is a reminder that success comes to those who refuse to give up, no matter how tough the journey gets.

Life, as I've learned, will always test you. But the real success lies in how you rise after every fall. As I look back, I realise that every struggle was worth it because it shaped me into the person I am today.

Regards,
Shivam

SHIVANGI'S STORY

Hello, Dear Readers,

Let's start with a story – the story of a normal girl with dreams to change the world.

I came into this world along with my twin brother. He is my biggest supporter and the person I love the most. I can't explain how much he means to me.

In class eight, my English teacher was telling us about Sir Ratan Tata – how he is changing the world with his work and making it a better place for others. When I told my teacher I would change the world one day, the whole class started laughing at me. However, my teacher came to me and told me, 'If you want to, you will'.

Years passed. We were in Class 10 preparing for our Boards. After my pre-Boards, when my tuition teacher saw my result, he just asked me, 'What is your goal?' I told him I wanted to change the world and make it a much better and safer place for others, including animals. Then, he told me that I needed to start with myself, if I wanted to change the world. If I had the ability to change myself, he said, I would have the ability to change the world.

As a Science Student, I expected to perform well on my 12th Boards. My score disappointed me, and I was upset. It felt like nothing was left, and I was finished. Then, my brother told me that my score would not decide what I was capable of doing in my life. Keeping his words in mind, I decided to take a drop year and prepare for the medical entrance exam.

I got admitted into Clinical Research in my undergraduation and I was also the best tennis player at my university.

This, though, was just half of my life. The real change came when I completed my UG Course as a Clinical Researcher. Now, it was time for higher studies. In my mind, I had the idea of becoming a doctor to serve society better. Thus, I decided to pursue an MD degree. First, I joined as a junior researcher while preparing for the medical entrance exam (MCAT), which I cracked after two years of work.

Finally, I got accepted to my dream university. This was not easy as I had to manage many things – my studies, extracurricular activities, research, and social work, along with my part-time job. I could manage all this, thanks to my family, friends, professors, and other amazing people I have met till now.

After completing my MD Course, professors at the university, some friends, and I organised health fairs in local places, teaching them about diet and hygiene, first-aid, and continually doing research to write informative articles and educate the public about health issues. This experience was amazing as it showed me that I was realising my aim of being in a position where I could help people and make the world a better place, something I hope to take much further in the years to come.

Regards,
Shivangi

SHRADDHA'S STORY

Dear Reader,

My life has been a little complicated from the beginning, but my father's support and confidence have always given me the courage to move ahead. When I was two years old, a person came into my life, someone who made my family complete: my sister. After her arrival, everything started looking perfect. But no one ever knows what will happen in life. Just two months after my sister's arrival, my mother died, and we reduced in number from four to three. Now, our father was everything for us.

However, our father himself was emotionally weak, and with time we got older, without realising how our lives had changed. Then, another big change came: our father got married for the second time. I thought that now our family would be complete, but this hope was also shattered. Life became more difficult as we had to leave our home, school, and friends and move to Mumbai.

During the time of COVID, when everyone was losing their jobs and homes, our entire world changed. It was very difficult to adjust to a new house, a new city, and a new way of life. Papa's support was there, but the family's condition became worse. It took time for our new Mummy to accept us, and we were struggling to fit into the new environment. There were fights and misunderstandings every day, but there was still hope that everything would be alright.

After school life, when I stepped into college life, I understood that in the world, there are people with even bigger problems than ours who learn to live happily. Seeing this, I understood that there is always a new path to rise above our struggles and live our lives proudly.

Then, the Udaan India Foundation entered my life. After coming here, I understood the purpose of my life. Udaan showed me how crucial it is to have confidence in one's self, and how to look at life from a new perspective. Udaan became my second family, where I found love, support, and guidance. Thanks to Udaan, I felt as if my parents were with me, as Udaan was my support and showed me that I could do anything in the world.

My dream now is to do something like this for children who are separated from their parents or whose parents have left everything and have sacrificed their lives for their children's studies. I want to do something for those parents and support those children's education so they can chase their dreams.

Thank you,
Shraddha

SHRUTI'S STORY

Dear Reader,

I'm pursuing a Master's degree in advanced accountancy. I like to read books, and I'm reading a lot about self-growth and self-development

Most of all, I'm exploring and working on what to do to make my dreams come true!

I would like to share an incident from my life. After this incident, I started feeling grateful!

When I was in the second year of college, I was facing medical issues. When I got it checked, I found out I had a stone in my gall bladder, which had no treatment. They said that an operation, along with blood tests, x-rays, etc, would have to be done because the size of the stone was more than normal. In government hospitals, dates are given to come for checking. I had to stand in queues almost from morning till afternoon, which was emotionally and physically straining. After the operation, I was not conscious, and my father was tense and crying. As we get older, we become different from our parents, though deep inside, we know that they love us. That day, I also learned that my father loves me a lot!

When there was pain, I used to cry and then Mummy also used to cry along with me and used to say, 'I can't see you like this'. Our mothers always love us, no matter how old we become.

During this journey, I always felt sad and became very silent. I don't know why, but it was so hard for me. When I was in the hospital, I saw that there were many problems in people's lives. Some had lost their loved ones, while others were just sitting, praying for the ones they loved. It was very overwhelming and made me feel grateful for what I have in my life.

At school, in many classes, only the chapter is taught and some standard questions and answers are given. We keep repeating this without a thought. I used to do the same thing – memorising all the answers, then going and writing it all in the exam, and soon forgetting everything. Then, in one of the classes, I understood that it is not just about rote learning – understanding concepts is also important. By understanding the concepts, we appreciate the meaning of the concept, why it is being taught to us, and why we should learn it. Then, I started evolving, trying to present concepts in my own words. I'm still learning how to do this. Studies became a little easier for me when I started understanding concepts. It was a great feeling to grasp the content instead of just rote learning. The biggest thing is that studies don't feel like a burden anymore, and I now understand all the concepts and present everything in my own words.

I used to be very afraid of writing papers. When I was in 10th grade, I had a teacher who took tests immediately after teaching everything. As this process was repeated, the fear of giving papers left my mind. Whenever I had a paper, it felt good because I would try to understand and implement the concept. I started enjoying this process.

I turned my weakness into strength! I was always a person who ran away from papers and tests, but as I gave every paper or class test, this fear of mine got completely finished.

I used to think Udaan India Foundation offered computer classes that prepared you for the digital world, but when I stepped into the classes, I realised it was not about computer skills but about building confidence, preparing for the real world, working on communication skills, and making us a better version of ourself. We learned a lot of things from Didi and Bhaiya.

One thing that feels really good is that everyone is called Didi and Bhaiya. This way, there is an emotional connection with them, and it feels like they are ours. They all talk so kindly and politely that it feels like everyone is very close. They taught, guided, and prepared us for everything, and I'm very grateful that I have started my journey with Udaan to give Udaan (flight) to my dreams. Udaan is full of positive vibes.

One thing I would like to change about the world is how people talk to each other – they should talk politely and respectfully, irrespective of who is in front of them and their age, clothes, or work.

Some pieces of advice based on my experience would be:

1. Always stay with your family, especially your parents, no matter what – they have always been there for you:)
2. Keep working on your skills. It helps!
3. Don't give up on your goals and passions.
4. Don't take anything for granted. Once it is gone, it will never come back.
5. No need to have a big circle of friends, if you have one friend who is always there for you, tells you your mistakes, helps you to grow, and tries to make you understand everything. These qualities are the most important.
6. Always learn the concept; don't go for rote learning! This helps you grow.

I always feel very grateful in my life for everything – everything from my surroundings, my family, and my best friend, to my food and clothes. I am grateful for the life I have!

Sometimes, the whole sky is full of darkness. But only after the night does the morning come.

Regards,
Shruti

SHUBHAVANI'S STORY

Dear Reader,

I often find myself reflecting on the most memorable and inspiring chapter of my life, which, without a doubt, is my journey with the Udaan India Foundation. I am deeply grateful to God for surrounding me with such helpful and inspiring individuals. This story is a celebration of the cherished memories I have made and the invaluable support I have received throughout this transformative experience.

Where I am today may not seem like a huge achievement to others, but it holds immense significance to me. If I look back five years ago, I could never have imagined that I would be able to speak English fluently, deliver presentations confidently in front of large audiences, and do several other things I do easily now.

For many, these might seem like small, everyday tasks, but for me, they have been milestones. Joining Udaan not only helped me develop my English skills but also allowed me to grow in countless other ways, becoming more independent and confident.

I remember feeling disheartened during my junior college days, watching others converse effortlessly in English. After my first year of college, I heard about Udaan and joined it with the simple goal of improving my English. What I discovered, however, was that Udaan was a nurturing environment that offered far more than language skills. It became a place where I received support for academic challenges and personal hurdles alike.

One of the most valuable lessons I learned came from Anurag Bhaiya, who once said, *'Jahan mauka mile, confidence se bolo* (Speak with confidence whenever you get the chance)'. This advice stuck with me and profoundly impacted my life. Another source of inspiration was my Udaan Didi, whose words, *'Agar tum kuch shiddat se chaaho to duniya usko milane mein lag jaati hai* (If you truly desire something, the world conspires to bring it to you)', motivated me to pursue my dreams with passion. Additionally, Shailesh Bhaiya's emphasis on punctuality has ingrained in me a strong sense of timeliness that continues to benefit me in my professional life.

However, Priya Ma'am had the most significant influence on my journey. I vividly recall the challenging times during my second year of college, when I had to balance classes, an internship, and classes at Udaan. My days began at 6 am, and by the time I reached the Udaan centre in the evening, I would be physically and mentally exhausted. There were moments when I felt overwhelmed, but Priya Ma'am was always there to uplift me. Her words, 'Be like a Rolls Royce, something different from everyone', gave me the strength and confidence to persevere.

My two-year journey with Udaan was filled with excitement, growth, and countless learning experiences. The foundation provided me with opportunities like access to laptops and valuable internships, which were instrumental in my development. I also had the privilege of meeting Malathi Ma'am, whose support and encouragement left a lasting impact on my life.

So, at the end, I want to say that Udaan India Foundation was not just a place to learn; it was where I found my confidence, voice, and passion. These cherished memories will always remain close to my heart, and I will forever be grateful to the people who helped me become who I am and reach where I am today.

Thank You,
Shubhavani

Srujal's Story

Dear Reader,

In 2018, my father suffered a paralysis attack, and our family struggled financially as all our savings would go toward his medical bills. Despite his poor health, he soon returned to work out of necessity, which took a toll on him.

In 2021, he had to undergo bypass surgery due to rising stress levels. During both crises, as the eldest child, I had to step up and manage home responsibilities while balancing school. My studies suffered, especially during 11th grade.

Although my father's health continues to decline, he still works under difficult conditions with no salary increase or company support. He is nearing retirement, and I know the responsibility of supporting my family will soon fall on me. I've decided to focus on my studies to improve our situation, but I worry about not being fully ready for what's ahead.

I have learned a lot of things from my life's journey. The challenges have been tough, and there are many I am yet to face, but I have learned that there's always hope; the way my father can manage everything in his condition inspires and motivates me.

Udaan is teaching me a lot of things. It has also built my confidence, giving me the motivation to write my story here. I am thankful to Udaan and grateful for its support.

Regards,

Srujal

TUSHAR'S STORY

I'm a 17-year-old boy living in Mumbai. I have always been known for my determination and hardworking nature. Life was challenging for me, but I've always had big dreams. My father was an auto-rickshaw driver who worked tirelessly to support the family and ensure that I could go to college and build a better future.

One unfortunate day, tragedy struck. My father passed away suddenly, leaving the family devastated. Not only did they lose the person they loved most, but they also lost their only source of income. I was still in college and knew that the weight of the family's survival had now fallen on my shoulders.

With no other option, I took up my father's work. Every day, before and after college, I would drive my father's auto-rickshaw through the busy streets, picking up passengers, earning just enough to keep the household running. It was exhausting – juggling college classes, assignments, and the long hours of work – but I was not one to give up easily. My eyes were set on a bigger dream, one that went beyond the rickshaw and the streets I knew so well.

Despite the hardships, I excelled in studies. My friends and Udaan India Foundation admired my grit, knowing I wasn't just a student but also the sole breadwinner for my family. While my classmates talked about going out, I would quietly slip away to start my shift, never complaining but always hopeful.

Years passed, and after countless sleepless nights and long, tiring days, I finally graduated from college. It was a proud moment for me and my family. But my aspirations were even higher. I applied for jobs in various companies, not content with just settling for the first opportunity that came my way.

Through sheer persistence and resilience, I eventually landed a job at a Crisil Limited company. The same boy who had once driven an auto rickshaw, balancing his books on the passenger seat during quiet moments, was now working in a modern office, wearing a suit and tie. I was on my way to fulfilling the dreams I had once only dared to imagine.

My journey has been far from easy, but it is a reminder that no matter how difficult life becomes, with enough effort and perseverance, even the loftiest of dreams can come true.

Tushar

UJALA'S STORY

Dear Reader,

In a small, modest house where dreams were as humble as the roof over our heads, I lived with my family. Our life was a testament to the quiet strength and resilience of the middle class. My father, the family's sole breadwinner, worked tirelessly at small jobs to keep the household running. But when COVID-19 turned the world upside down, it brought new, harsh challenges.

During the lockdown, my father took on a gruelling job as a delivery boy, working around the clock. Every day, we held our breath, fearing for his safety. When he came home, the sight of his chapped, red hands was a painful reminder of his relentless struggle. My heart ached as I saw the physical toll on him, and I vowed to change our story.

I imagined a future where my father could relax in a big house, sipping tea without a worry in the world.

Despite these hardships, I excelled academically, finishing my tenth grade with 83 per cent. My father, though facing his own trials, celebrated my achievement with a box of sweets. He was proud of my success and saw it as defying those who doubted the value of educating daughters. His pride in my success was a poignant contrast to our difficult circumstances.

Our struggles intensified. When my grandfather passed away, my father couldn't afford the last-minute flight to the village. Financial strains, exacerbated by the pandemic, led to the sale of our home and left us vulnerable to creditors and unkind remarks. Even my father's own brothers, focused on their share of the house, offered no support.

In the midst of this turmoil, I witnessed my father's deep sorrow, including his tears on my birthday and his thoughts of despair. But rather than succumbing to the weight of our situation, my resolve hardened. I was determined to transform our fate and prove that educating daughters was not in vain.

My dream is not just to make my father proud but to show that every girl has the potential to overcome obstacles and achieve greatness. I want to be a beacon of hope, demonstrating that with dedication and hard work, dreams could turn into reality. I aspire to bring joy and security to my family, inspiring others to believe in the power of their own potential.

In my pursuit of this vision, I aim to embody the spirit of resilience and hope, proving that even in the face of adversity, determination can light the way to a brighter future.

Regards,
Ujala

VIDYASAGAR'S STORY

Hi.

I always wanted to be an army officer. But my father wanted me to study hotel management. I tried it, but I didn't like it. I felt like I was doing something that wasn't right for me.

I decided to leave the course, but my family was upset. They thought I was making a mistake. We argued a lot, but I knew I had to follow my own path.

Then, I discovered aviation. I loved the thrill of flying and the feeling of freedom. I knew I had to pursue it, so I enrolled in an aviation course.

But, again, I felt like something was missing. I left the aviation course, and my family was furious. They thought I was wasting my life, changing my mind all the time.

But I knew I had to keep searching for what was right for me. That's when I discovered my passion for banking and insurance. I decided to study Bachelor of Banking and Insurance (BBI). It felt like the right fit.

My family was sceptical at first, but I'm determined to make it work. I'm finally doing something I love and won't give up. I know I've made mistakes, but I'm learning from them. I'm finding my own way, and that's all that matters.

Regards,
Vidyasagar

Yuvraj's Story

Dear Reader,

Hello.

I was born in Mumbai in 2005. At the time of my birth, my mother had to undergo an operation, which caused her significant health issues. My two elder brothers had been born without any major complications, but after I was born, my mother's health began to deteriorate. She had to undergo a neck operation. My father had moved to Mumbai from Punjab in 2002, and initially, we lived in a rental home.

In 2012, my uncle built two houses, one of which was given to my dad. From 2002 to 2008, my father worked as a car driver. In 2008, he managed to buy a second-hand truck, which helped our financial situation. However, in 2014, my eldest brother had to undergo an appendix operation, and as the three of us grew up, our expenses started to increase.

I did well academically up until the 8th grade, passing with ease, but when I reached the 9th grade, I struggled and failed in four subjects: Geometry, Algebra, Geography, and History. Then, the COVID-19 pandemic hit, and due to the lockdown, I was promoted to the next grade without giving Board exams. This was a bit of a let-down, because the failure in 9th grade had actually pushed me to study hard during the lockdown. I had spent six days a week, six hours a day, locked in a room, preparing for my 10th-grade exams. I had everything memorized

–from math formulas to the periodic table. After all of that, my Board exams got cancelled.

Then, I enrolled at a college in Bhandup, where I completed my 11th and 12th grades in the Commerce stream. It was a challenging journey, but I managed to complete my education despite the many obstacles my family and I faced.

During my summer holiday, I decided to join Udaan, initially thinking it was just a regular computer class. But I didn't know that this experience would turn out to be a much bigger journey, one that would span over one and a half years. When I first started, I didn't anticipate the depth and variety of skills I would learn, nor did I expect the personal growth that would come along with it.

I began by completing my basic course under the guidance of Anurag sir, who made learning both engaging and insightful. Once I finished my basic training, I moved on to the Prep programme, which further deepened my understanding of IT and business processes. After that, I decided to dive into Digital Marketing, again under Anurag sir's mentorship. While I initially thought Digital Marketing would enhance my marketing skills, something unexpected happened – it wasn't just my marketing knowledge that grew. What really skyrocketed were my confidence, patience, and ability to deliver presentations. These soft skills took me to a whole new level, and I could feel the transformation in the way I carried myself.

Udaan also provided opportunities to visit several well-known companies, such as Teleperformance, Marsh McLennan, and LinkedIn. These visits gave me first-hand experience of the corporate world, showing me how things work behind the scenes in large organisations. It was eye-opening and a significant milestone in my learning journey, helping me understand the practical aspects of business and communication.

During this time, after 12th grade, I was admitted into college. However, after some time, I felt a strong urge to take a break and drop out for a while. I can't pinpoint the exact reason why I made that decision, but I felt it was necessary.

Nevertheless, I'm determined to continue my studies next year, with a clearer sense of direction and purpose.

Regards,
Yuvraj

UNNATI'S STORY

Dear Reader,

I am a bubbly girl who doesn't like to stress about life. I enjoy having fun, and I know how to find joy in whatever I'm doing. So, let me talk about my background. I come from a Maharashtrian family. There are four people in my family -my brother, my mother, my grandmother, and me. My mother is a single parent, raising me and my older brother with great care.

When it comes to my dreams and hopes, my dream is to become an independent woman in my life, not just financially but also mentally. This is because financial independence can be achieved by working as much as you live, but staying emotionally strong and independent is much more important to me. My hope is that just as a sea is made up of many drops, I at least want to see 10 women in my community or friend circle become independent, not just

After completing 12th grade, I got my first job as an admission counsellor, where I worked with children and understood their mindsets. At that time, Udaan allowed me to work with them. It's been one and a half years since I started working with them. If I talk about what I'm proud of, it's that I have managed two batches so far, with a total of 60 children under my guidance.

Currently, I am handling two batches with around 50+ children. Proudly, I can say that 20 of these new children joined because of recommendations from my previous students. This feels like a ripple effect to me. Just as ripples spread outward when a stone is thrown into a pond, the recommendations from my students have created a similar effect. I am very proud of this. Life is a staircase of continuous progression; with each step, we create ripples of impact and gather knowledge to fuel our climb.

Life will undoubtedly bring many challenges, and we haven't faced many yet. But if I had to describe my life in one word, it would be "progression." We must keep moving forward, but we don't know what challenges or opportunities lie ahead. When we're young, we often think our older siblings have perfect lives m and we want to grow up to be like them. But once we become like them, we realize there's always more to achieve Similarly, in life, we don't know how many hurdles we'll face, but everyone is motivated to keep climbing that staircase.

Just as my Udaan family is always there for me, there are also many others who are ready to help. When it comes to what to learn in life, I think of the movie *3 idiots*, which features three friends—Farhan, Raju, and Rancho. On their first day of college, rancho says, "har jagah gyan but raha hai balak jahan se mile lete chalo jahan na mile aage badho aur jahan mil raha hai vahan se le lo" "Go where knowledge is available, take as much as you can. Knowledge is everywhere; take it where you find it, and move on if it's not available."

This is my learning philosophy as well: take in as much knowledge as you can wherever you find it.

Thank you!

Unnati

JUHI'S STORY

Dear Reader,

I was once a shy and underconfident girl, struggling to use even simple English words. Expressing myself to others felt impossible, and I believed confidence and fluency were dreams which I wouldn't be able to achieve. But after finishing 10th grade in 2018, I decided to work on myself.

It wasn't easy as I was scared to speak and afraid of making mistakes. However, I faced my fears and focused on improving my English and confidence. Step by step, I practiced speaking, reading, and writing, learning from every mistake and never giving up. Joining Udaan India Foundation was a turning point. They encouraged me to aim higher and believe in myself. With their support, I transformed from a shy girl into a confident girl.

I began speaking in sessions and meetings without worrying about being judged, which helped me overcome my fear. This experience taught me that setting goals and working hard will make anything achievable.

Today, I am proud to say I am an engineer, something I thought I would never be able to achieve. The journey wasn't just about academics as I grew emotionally and mentally, learning to believe in myself. Now I dream of helping others who lack confidence or resources to achieve their goals just as I did.

I want everyone to know that no matter what you face, keep pushing forward. You can achieve your dreams and with the right guidance and hard work, you can turn them into reality.

With determination and gratitude,
Juhi

Priyanka's Story

During my college degree, I found myself searching for meaningful ways to start my career. In 2022, I came across the Udaan India Foundation, a place that seemed like a perfect fit for my learning. My first program at Udaan was Basic Literacy, where I was fortunate to learn from Priya Ma'am, one of my favourite teachers. She didn't just teach lessons; she inspired me with her passion and dedication to making a difference. It was a great way to begin my journey.

I interned at Udaan for six months, and during that time, I learned so much more than I ever imagined. It wasn't just about helping kids learn, but also about understanding their struggles and offering them a sense of hope. The experience made me realize how powerful education can be in shaping lives, and I'm incredibly grateful to Udaan for allowing me to be part of something so impactful. Those six months were truly a turning point for me, and I carry the lessons I learned there with me every day.

However, after my internship, I went through a challenging phase. For four months, I wasn't doing anything work-related, and that uncertainty was difficult to navigate. I didn't know what direction to take next, and at times, it felt frustrating. But during this time, I found something valuable: spending time with my family. We are five members, and the time I spent with them during those months was precious. Their constant support, understanding, and encouragement gave me the strength to keep going. Looking back, I see that period as a time of personal growth, where I learned the importance of patience and family.

Eventually, things took a positive turn when I got an opportunity to intern at General Mills in the supply chain team, thanks to my experience at Udaan. The corporate world was a whole new experience, but I was eager to learn and challenge myself. Working at General Mills has been an eye-opener in many ways. I've gained insights into how supply chains operate and how different pieces come together to make things run smoothly. Every day, I'm learning new skills that I know will be valuable as I move forward in my career.

While work keeps me busy, I've always made sure to stay connected with my passions outside of my professional life. One of my greatest joys is traveling and spending time in nature. There's something about being outdoors that refreshes and energizes me. I've travelled to several places, but one of my favourite trips was trekking at Tungeshwar. It was a thrilling experience, walking through the trails and being surrounded by nature's beauty. Trekking gives me a sense of peace and adventure, and I try to make time for it whenever I can.

Looking ahead, I know there's still so much to explore, both in my career and in life. I want to continue pushing myself, learning new things, and growing as a person. I believe every experience teaches us something valuable. I'm excited to see where the future takes me and I am always ready for new challenges and opportunities that come my way.

Thank you!

Priyanka

TULSI'S STORY

Born into a humble family in a small town, I was raised with strong values and a simple lifestyle. One of the core principles instilled in me from a young age was being a pure vegetarian. This was not just a dietary choice but a reflection of our faith, culture, and the respect we held for all living beings.

Life, for the most part, was blissful. I was a bright student who excelled academically, even in a Hindi-medium school. My consistent performance made my parents immensely proud, and their pride became my source of inspiration. However, during my 12th grade, just as I was preparing for the most crucial exams of my life, fate threw an unexpected challenge my way.

It all began when I allowed a few new friends into my life. They appeared supportive and friendly at first, but their influence turned out to be harmful. One day, they insisted I eat meat. At first, I resisted vehemently, explaining my lifelong commitment to being a vegetarian. However, their relentless pressure and taunts broke my resolve, and I gave in, a decision I deeply regretted almost immediately.

The consequences were swift and severe. Within hours, I began to feel extremely unwell. Nausea turned into persistent vomiting, and my health deteriorated rapidly. To make matters worse, a painful lump developed in my throat. When I was rushed to the hospital, the doctors diagnosed it as a severe allergic reaction exacerbated by stress. They prescribed 18 months of medication, alongside other treatments, to restore my health.

This crisis unfolded at the worst possible time—right before my 12th-grade board exams. I was at a crossroads. Should I prioritize my health, or should I focus on my studies? It felt like an impossible decision. Yet, deep down, I knew I could not give up on either. Despite the physical and emotional toll, I resolved to fight. My faith in Lord Narayan and Shri Krishna became my anchor. I prayed for strength and guidance, and with their blessings, I found the courage to tackle both my health challenges and my studies simultaneously.

The months that followed were incredibly challenging. Hospital visits, medication side effects, and surgery consumed much of my time and energy. But I refused to let these obstacles deter me. Every free moment I had, I dedicated to my studies. Post-surgery, I had only one month to prepare for the exams. Many people advised me to take a gap year, but I chose otherwise. My belief in myself and the divine kept me going.

When the results were announced, I wasn't among the top scorers, but I had passed. To the world, my achievement might have seemed ordinary, but to me, it was extraordinary. It symbolized my victory over despair, doubt, and adversity. I knew in my heart that it was the blessings of Shri Krishna and Lord Narayan that had guided me through those dark times.

After my exams, I secured admission to a reputable degree college. This achievement was another milestone in my journey of resilience. Today, I am working tirelessly to build a bright future for myself, driven by the lessons my journey has taught me.

This story is not just about surviving illness or resisting negative influences; it is about staying true to one's values, finding strength in faith, and facing life's challenges head-on.

Thank you!

Tulsi

ABOUT UDAAN INDIA FOUNDATION

Udaan India Foundation (Udaan) is a Mumbai-based not-for-profit organisation working with children from low-income communities in the field of education. Our primary aim is to ensure that every child of school-going age is gaining a strong and holistic educational foundation to become a responsible, compassionate and confident citizen of tomorrow.

Most Udaan children are from families where there has been little or no formal education, where education is not a priority and it is a common place for children to drop out of school in order to contribute to the family income. Believing in the power of education to change lives, a child's journey at Udaan starts at the Kindergarten level, continues through school years and supports them until they become employable. The focus is always in making learning a continuous, joyous and voluntary experience that will help the children discover and achieve their true potential and take on the future with confidence. In 2024, Udaan completed 20 years of serving the local community through its efforts.

Through our work we strive to see the following perceptible changes:

Short term

- Enhanced academic performance
- Decrease in drop-out rate

Intermediate term

- Increased enrolment in higher education
- Enhanced employability skills

Long term

- Meaningful employment
- Self-sufficiency
- Responsible citizens

Learn more about us and how you can get involved at www.udaanindiafoundation.org.

ABOUT PROJECT KAHAANI

Steve Jobs once famously said, 'The most powerful man in the world is the storyteller'.

Storytelling isn't just about spinning yarns and entertaining others. Storytelling develops creativity, communication, and the confidence to get one's ideas out to others. Those are skills that are important not just to a writer but in a job interview, for the new employee seeking to shine at work, or the budding entrepreneur seeking to get his or her ideas heard by investors or customers.

Project Kahaani was founded by Aaditya Sengupta Dhar, a Mumbai-based student and author. It is a project started by a teenager, led by teens, and devoted to helping other teens give voice to their hopes and aspirations and succeed in achieving their aims through the power of storytelling and communication.

We operate on the belief that every single one of us has a story that deserves to be told, a voice that deserves to be heard, and that the world would be a better place if we took the time to hear and share each other's stories.

The mission of *Project Kahaani* is to empower teens from low-income communities whose stories would otherwise go unheard with the communication skills to get their stories out to the world and build the confidence and soft skills that will set them up for success in their lives.

Meet the all-teen team at Project Kahaani:

Aaditya Sengupta Dhar

Ahmed Nensey

Ali Syed

Rajveer Vohra

Veer Ajbani

Vihaan Jain

Yohann Jain

ABOUT AADITYA SENGUPTA DHAR

Aaditya Sengupta Dhar, the founder of *Project Kahaani*, has had a passion for storytelling and writing since he was very young. His first 'book' was a handwritten encyclopaedia of ancient civilizations written when he was eight, and seeing it displayed in the school library motivated him to keep writing. He wrote his first fantasy novel *Secret Tails (2019)* when he was ten. His next novel, *Legend of the Broken Blade* (2023), was acclaimed as one of the 'Top 15 must-read books of 2023' (The Morning Standard).

Aaditya aspires to use his writing to make a positive difference. His 2021 eBook, *Underdogs*, inspired readers to help underprivileged children unleash their potential, with sales proceeds donated to Save The Children India. His short story, *Tug of War* (2021), about teens finding common ground among communal tensions, won first prize in the Melton Global Storytelling Contest. His 2022 book, *Back from the Brink*, based on research funded by a micro-grant he won from MIT Solv[ED], highlighted the issue of urban animal extinction and how we can make a difference. *The Teen's Guide to Saving the World* (2023), an Amazon India bestseller, inspired teens to create a positive impact, winning multiple international awards, including Silver Medal at the Non-Fiction Book Awards in the US, Silver Medal at the Reader's Favorite Awards in the US, and Top 3 Global Finalist at the Teen Reader's Choice Awards, the only major literary award in the US where nominations and voting are done entirely by teens.

His latest novel *Kaalchakra* (2024), an Amazon bestseller, reconnects Indian youth with their cultural roots and heritage. A short story on this theme won a Gold Finalist Award at the prestigious Queen's Commonwealth Essay Competition in 2023.

Aaditya is the creator of the *Vedanomics* column on BW Businessworld, where he writes articles highlighting inspiration we can take from our past in the world of economics and business, and hosts the *Vedanomics* podcast on Spotify, where he interviews CXOs to explore how Indian values and philosophy create a uniquely Indian approach to leadership.

For his efforts in making a positive impact through his writing, Aaditya was awarded the Young Achievers Award in 2024 by the Indian Achievers' Forum, an apex national body.

When not writing, Aaditya focuses on excelling at school, follows Cricket with a passion, and practices Karate, in which he holds a black belt. Aaditya is sixteen years old and lives in Mumbai.